THE
Calligrapher's
PROJECT BOOK

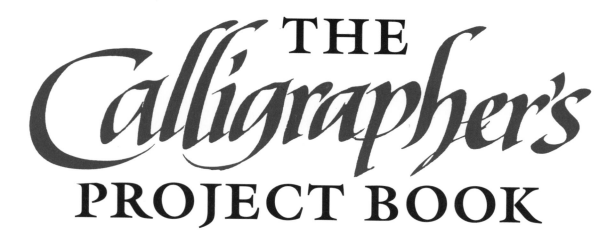

THE Calligrapher's PROJECT BOOK

SUSANNE HAINES

PROJECTS BY

Irena Armstrong
Brenda Berman
Lindsay Castell
Gerald Fleuss
Patricia Gidney
Gaynor Goffe
Susan Hufton
Lilly Lee
Christine Oxley
Andrew Parkinson
Tom Perkins

HarperCollins*Publishers*

First published in hardback in 1987 by
William Collins Sons & Co Ltd
London · Glasgow · Sydney
Auckland · Toronto · Johannesburg
First published in paperback 1989
Reprinted 1990
Reprinted by HarperCollins Publishers 1991, 1993 (three times), 1994

Please note that all names and addresses in the invitation,
printed stationery and logo are fictitious.

British Library Cataloguing in Publication Data
Haines, Susanne
The calligrapher's project book
1. Calligraphy & manuscript illumination – Manuals
I. Title
745.6

ISBN 0 00 412483-9

Typeset by Peter MacDonald, Twickenham
Printed in Singapore by Toppan

This book was edited, designed and produced by
The Paul Press Ltd.

Art Editors	ANTONY JOHNSON
	TONY PAINE
Project Editor	SALLY MACEACHERN
Photography	BILL BURNETT
Illustrations	IAN BOTT
Art Assistants	MICHAEL SNELL
	CLAIRE GILCHRIST
Index	RICHARD BIRD
Art Director	STEPHEN McCURDY
Editorial Director	JEREMY HARWOOD

CONTENTS

INTRODUCTION 6

GALLERY 8

MATERIALS AND PENMANSHIP 34

PRACTICAL CALLIGRAPHY 68

GLOSSARY 138

INDEX AND ACKNOWLEDGEMENTS 140

INTRODUCTION

Calligraphy: from the Greek – kalli (beauty), and graphia (write).

If you are attracted by the visual appeal of letter forms, if you like writing and are interested in words, if you have some time and some patience, a pen, paper and ink, then the art of calligraphy may appeal to you. Do not be deterred by a lack of natural artistic ability, for although this is undeniably an advantage, it is not essential: calligraphy is a skill that can be learnt.

The attraction of calligraphy today perhaps partly stems from a reaction against the rapid pace of our high-tech world. The physical sensation of using pen and ink on paper to create a unique expression of a letter, a word, or a text must surely afford greater satisfaction to many people than tapping at a keyboard, or scribbling a hurried note.

Enthusiasm for calligraphy continues to grow – not only in its formal approach and traditional uses, such as commemorative addresses, family trees, diplomas, and the like, but also in a freer, more expressive approach to the enjoyment and interpretation of the written word.

However, while there is a growing interest in calligraphy, there is at the same time a need for more teaching. Evening classes and residential courses play a very important part in nurturing interest in the craft; societies provide information, workshops and contact with other people; but there are few courses which specialize in calligraphy and lettering, or which even incorporate it into broader arts courses.

This book aims to provide a course which will enable you to teach yourself at home. It is arranged so that you can choose to follow the order of the book, or to structure your study to suit yourself; you can work at your own pace, and set your own level of achievement.

The first obvious problem when teaching yourself is how to begin. This is answered for you here in two ways: firstly, by providing a selection of examples in the "gallery" section of the book which will give you an idea of the variety of approaches that are possible. Secondly (after discussing the materials you will need), you are introduced in gradual stages to the basics of "penmanship". This reference section gives you all the basic information you will need. It encourages you to experiment with materials, and, when you are confident, to develop your own personal writing style.

The main section of the book enables you to apply your skills. Its most valuable aspect is that you are shown the planning stages for each piece of work (something which is normally impossible unless you are in a studio or classroom situation). Whether you follow the projects step-by-step "to the letter", or whether you use the ideas and techniques for your own designs, this insight into the varied working methods of a number of experienced calligraphers is an invaluable teaching aid.

Each project is designed to open up some new aspect of the craft, to suggest handy tips and shortcuts, and to simplify techniques, thus encouraging you to try your hand at a wide variety of skills. There is a series of projects which shows you how to prepare work for reproduction, in the hope that this will encourage you to think of making practical use of your work; however it is not essential to go through the printing process to enjoy the results. At times, the book deliberately sets out to sidetrack you – with techniques such as scraperboard and embossing. Some projects, such as heraldry, give you just a taste of a specialized subject which will repay further investigation. This diversity is designed to encourage you to view calligraphy within a much broader framework.

In your writing, aim for a rhythm, and for crisp, spontaneously written letters. In time, and with some effort, you will be able to achieve a natural, seemingly effortless control of the pen. A confident understanding of letters written with the edged pen will help you to understand the technique of drawn lettering, which is introduced towards the end of the book.

The satisfaction of calligraphy is as much in the viewing as in the doing. The contrast and liveliness of beautifully executed letters can evoke feelings of great pleasure in the viewer. And the actual making of the letters, when all the conditions are right, the pen is working, your hand is steady and your mind is calm, can take on a meditative quality. A sensitive response to the words and control over the pen and letter forms marks the beginning of a real understanding of the craft, and of the art of calligraphy.

One of the fascinating aspects of calligraphy is that it can lead you in many different directions: you may be quite content to enjoy it simply as a relaxing hobby; you may want to develop it as a commercial sideline, or even try to make a living out of it. You may find yourself becoming obsessed by the desire to attain very high standards of craftmanship, or to handcraft your own tools and materials, such as pens, inks, paints and paper. You may start studying the history of the development of letter forms, or illumination; discovering a whole new field of literature, or a subject of interest previously unfamiliar to you. It may inspire you to take up drawing, painting or illustration; study graphics and type design; or use letter forms in related crafts, such as fabrics or ceramics. The possibilities are endless...

SUSANNE HAINES

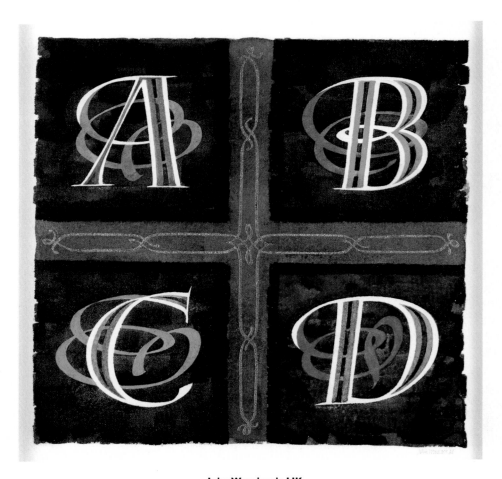

John Woodcock, UK

ABCD

152 × 152mm (6 × 6in)

Brush lettering on handmade paper, using
watercolour, inks, resist and gum ammoniac gilding.

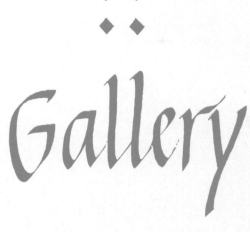

Gallery

This introductory section of recent work by practising calligraphers illustrates the broad range of approaches and techniques that are available to the calligrapher. It also demonstrates a varied use of materials, and a rich and exciting use of colour. Here you will find examples of work done purely for personal satisfaction, work specifically undertaken for exhibition, formal work done to commission, and printed work for both commercial and non-commercial use. The variety, skill and ingenuity of the work is an inspiration to the beginner and more experienced calligrapher alike.

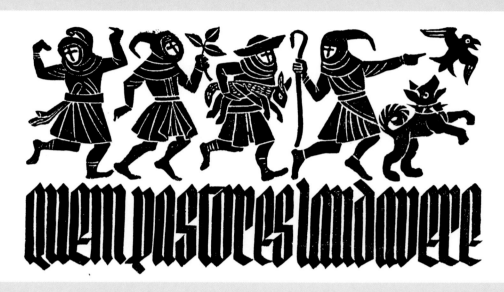

George L. Thomson, UK
CHRISTMAS CARD

85 × 110mm (3¼ × 4¼in)

Rubber stamp, using hand-cut pencil eraser,
printed with a hand press (hand pressure
alone is not enough for erasers of this size).

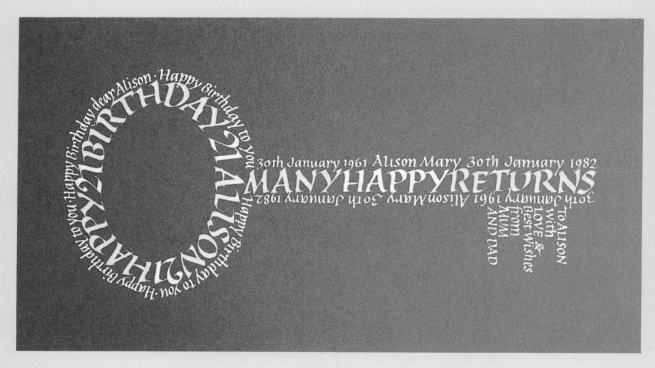

John Smith, UK
TWENTY-FIRST BIRTHDAY CARD

120 × 220mm (4¾ × 8½in)

Pen-lettering in designer's gouache on dark
green Daler board.

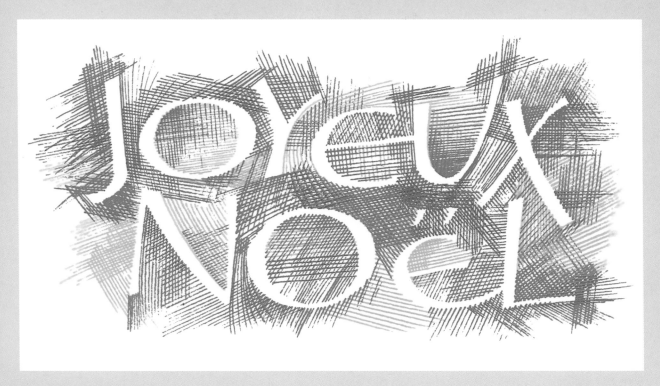

Stan Knight, UK

JOYEUX NOEL

100 × 170mm (4 × 6¾in)

Hand screen print in three colours on
Bockingford NOT pressed watercolour
paper. Print separations for the screens were
made by tracing over a preliminary pencil
crayon draft.

What wondrous love is this , O my soul , O my soul ,
What wondrous love is this , O my soul !
What wondrous love is this THE ETERNAL THEME
AMERICAN FOLK HYMN **That caused the Lord of bliss**
To lay aside his crown for my soul, for my soul
To lay aside his crown for my soul.

Susan Hufton, UK

CHRISTMAS CARD

85 × 205mm (3¼ × 8in)

Written in black ink, and printed in black,
some lines screened to give a tint.

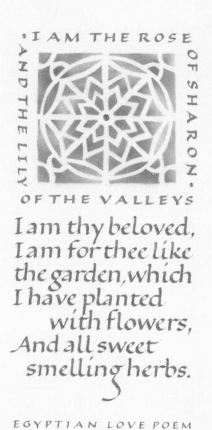

I AM THE ROSE OF SHARON·
·AND THE LILY OF THE VALLEYS

I am thy beloved,
I am for thee like
the garden, which
I have planted
   with flowers,
And all sweet
   smelling herbs.

EGYPTIAN LOVE POEM

Hazel Beney, UK
EGYPTIAN LOVE POEM

254 × 152mm (10 × 6in)

Written in gouache with metal
nibs. The stencil design was
airbrushed and the gold dots
gilded on gesso.

FROM GOULIES
AND GHOSTIES
AND LONGLEGGETTY
BEASTIES
AND THINGS
THAT GO BUMP
IN THE NIGHT
GOOD LORD DELIVER US!

Jane Addison, UK
GOOD LORD DELIVER US

148 × 140mm (6 × 5½in)

Lettering in red gouache and
Chinese ink stick.

CUMQUE MATURE SURREXISSET
TULIT DUAS UXORES SUAS ET
TOTIDEM FAMULAS CUM UNDECIM
FILIIS ET TRANSIVIT VADUM
IACOB·TRADUCTISQUE OMNIBUS
QUAE AD SE PERTINEBAT

MANSIT SOLUS ET
ECCE VIR LUCTABATUR
CUM EO USQUE MANO
Qui cum videret quod eum
superare non posset, tetigit
nervum eius femoris, et
statim emarcuit. Dixitque
ad eum: Dimitte me iam
enim ascendit aurora·Res-
pondit: Non dimittam te
nisi benedixeris mihi·An
ergo: Quod nomen est tibi?
Respondit: Iacob·At ille:
Nequaquam, inquit, Iacob
appellabitur nomen tuum
sed Israel: quoniam si contra
Deum fortis fuisti, quanto
magis contra homines
praevalebis? Interrogavit
eum Iacob: Dic mihi quo
appellaris nomine? Respondit:
Cur quaeris nomen meum?
Et benedixit ei in eodem
loco·Vocavitque Iacob nomen
loci illius Phanuel, dicens:

VIDI DEUM FACIE AD
FACIEM ET SALVA FACTA
EST ANIMA MEA
ORTUSQUE EST EI STATIM
SOL POSTQUAM TRANSGRES-
SUS EST PHANUEL· IPSE
VERO CLAUDICABAT PEDE
QUAM OB CAUSAM NON
COMEDUNT NERVUM FILII
ISRAEL QUI EMARCUIT IN
FEMORE IACOB USQUE
IN PRAESENTEM DIEM· EO
QUOD TETIGERIT NERVUM
FEMORIS EIUS ET OB·
STUPUERIT·

GENESIS 32

**Brody Neuenschwander,
USA**

PUGNA JACOB CUM ANGELO

74 × 30.6cm (29 × 12½in)

Gouache on Rives printmaking
paper, written with a quill, except
for the large capitals which were
done with a metal pen. The gold
of the cross was applied over a
mixture of gesso and PVA.

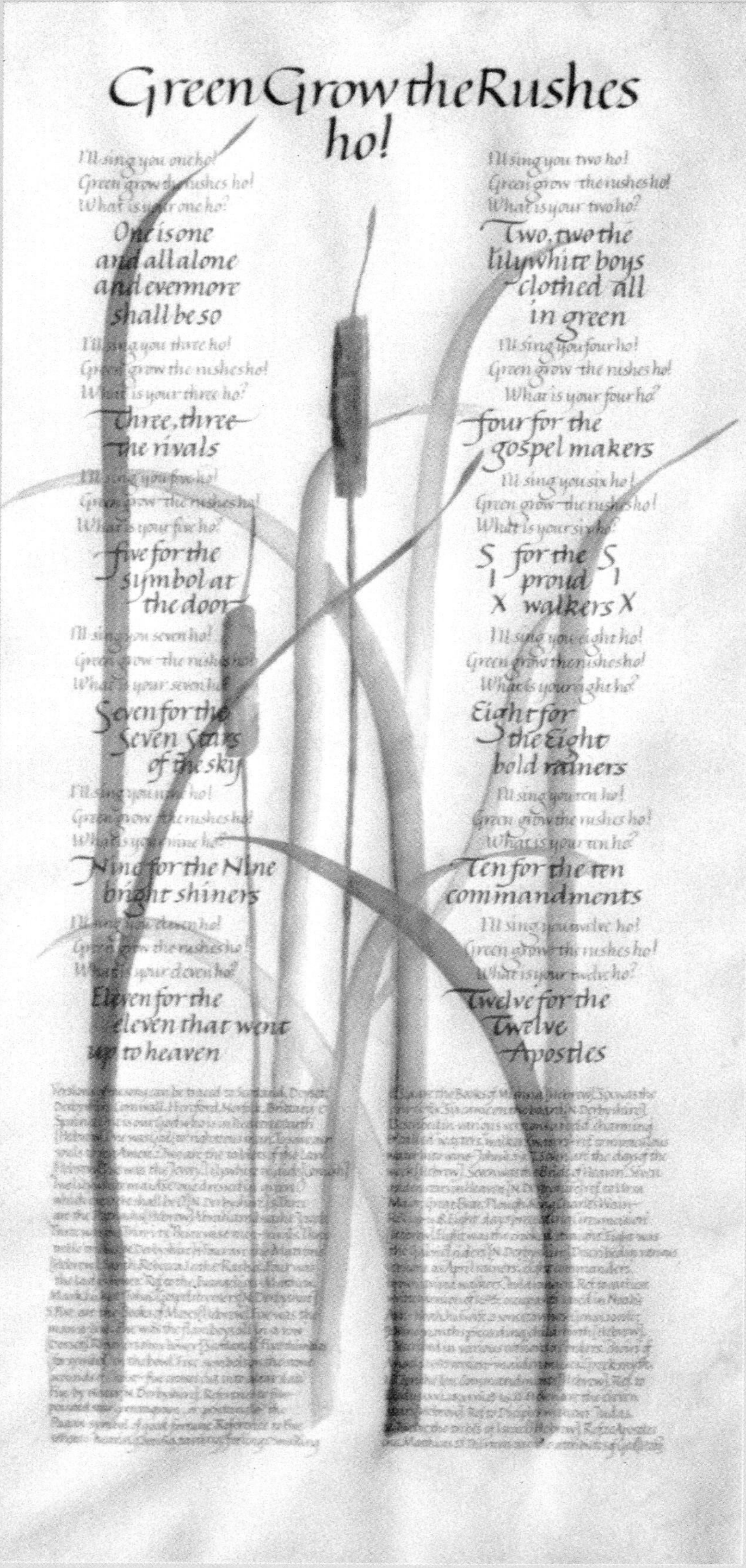

Christine Oxley, UK

GREEN GROW THE RUSHES HO!

71 × 42cm (28 × 16½in)

Gouache on vellum. Rushes painted with a chisel-edged brush; text written with metal pens.

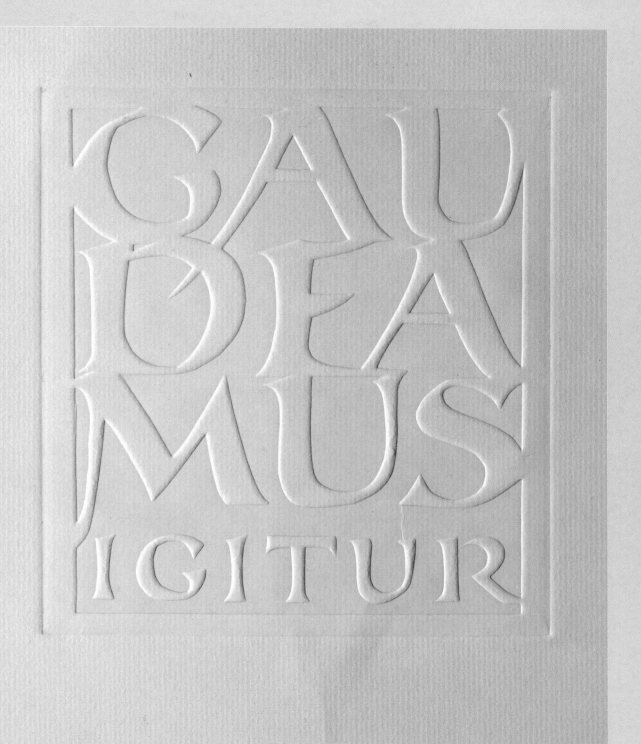

Celia Kilner, UK
GAUDEAMUS IGITUR

210 × 178mm (8¼ × 7¼in)

Pen-made letters (originally designed for a
terra cotta tile) acid-etched on to a zinc plate
and embossed on to Fabriano paper.

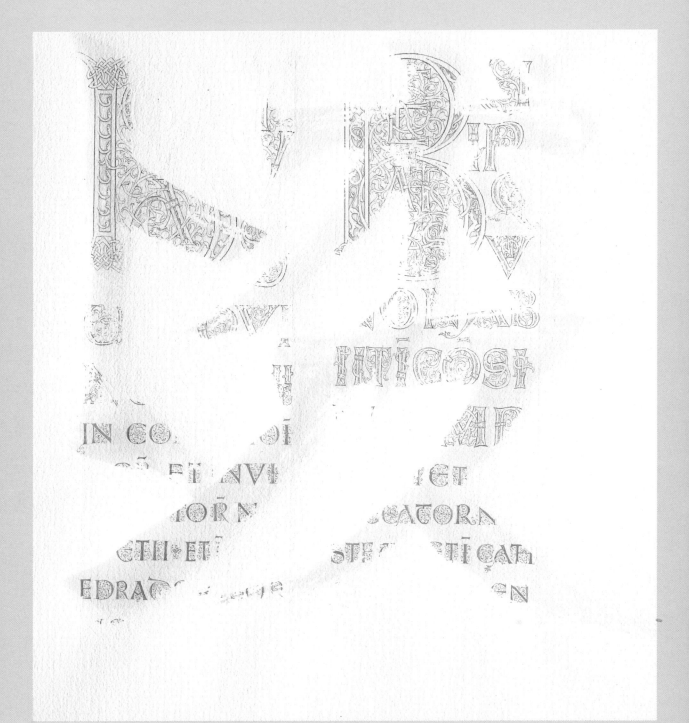

Mark Van Stone, USA
BOSTON BEATUS

53 × 51cm (21 × 20 in)

Palimpsest-like overlay of Japanese katakana characters for Boston,
over a 12th century-style double psalter (the first psalm begins
'Beatus vir qui non abiit'). The skeletal drawing for the psalter pages
was made with a stylus on Fabriano watercolour paper and the
Japanese characters were then brushed on in sepia. In these areas
the drawing was finished with ink and gouache.

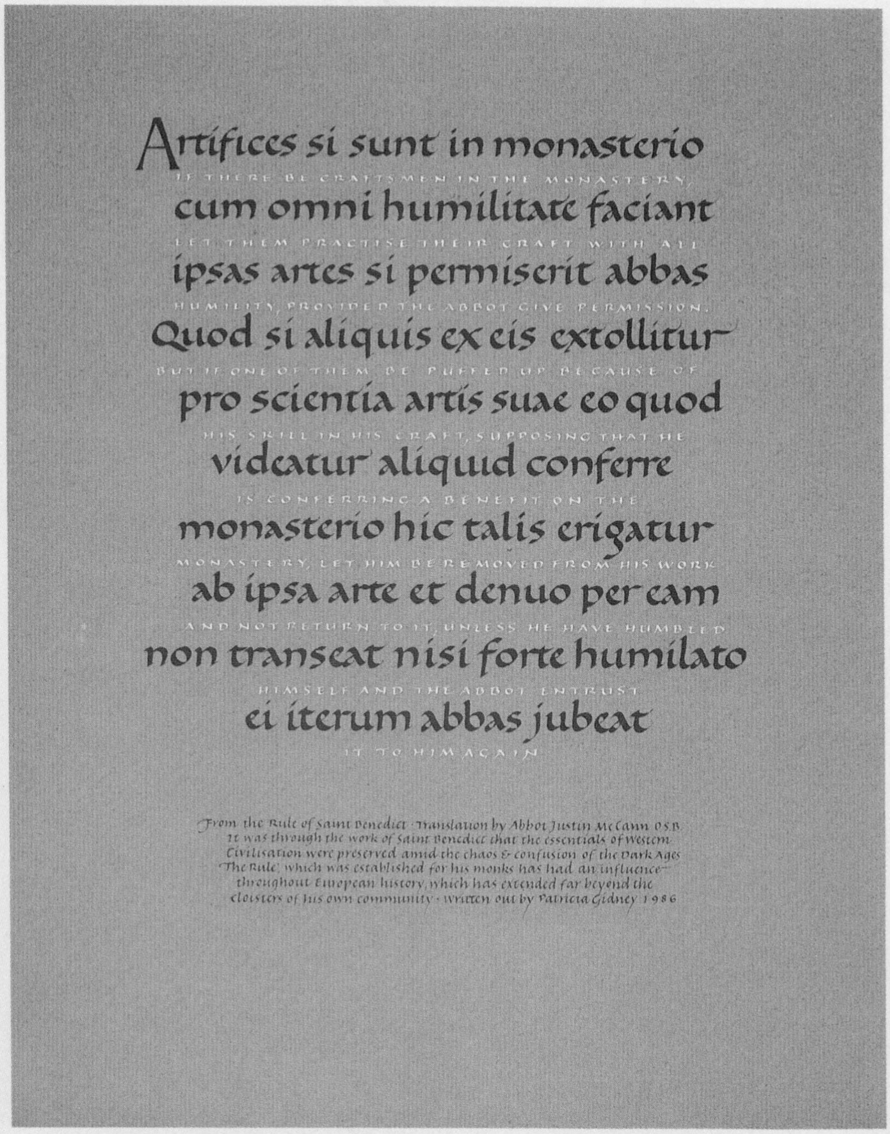

Artifices si sunt in monasterio
IF THERE BE CRAFTSMEN IN THE MONASTERY,
cum omni humilitate faciant
LET THEM PRACTISE THEIR CRAFT WITH ALL
ipsas artes si permiserit abbas
HUMILITY, PROVIDED THE ABBOT GIVE PERMISSION.
Quod si aliquis ex eis extollitur
BUT IF ONE OF THEM BE PUFFED UP BECAUSE OF
pro scientia artis suae eo quod
HIS SKILL IN HIS CRAFT, SUPPOSING THAT HE
videatur aliquid conferre
IS CONFERRING A BENEFIT ON THE
monasterio hic talis erigatur
MONASTERY, LET HIM BE REMOVED FROM HIS WORK
ab ipsa arte et denuo per eam
AND NOT RETURN TO IT, UNLESS HE HAVE HUMBLED
non transeat nisi forte humilato
HIMSELF AND THE ABBOT ENTRUST
ei iterum abbas jubeat
IT TO HIM AGAIN

From the Rule of Saint Benedict · Translation by Abbot Justin McCann OSB.
It was through the work of Saint Benedict that the essentials of Western
Civilisation were preserved amid the chaos & confusion of the Dark Ages
· The Rule, which was established for his monks has had an influence
throughout European history, which has extended far beyond the
cloisters of his own community · written out by Patricia Gidney 1986

Patricia Gidney, UK
QUOTATION FROM THE RULE OF ST
BENEDICT

406 × 305mm (16 × 12in)

Chinese ink and white gouache on
Ingres paper.

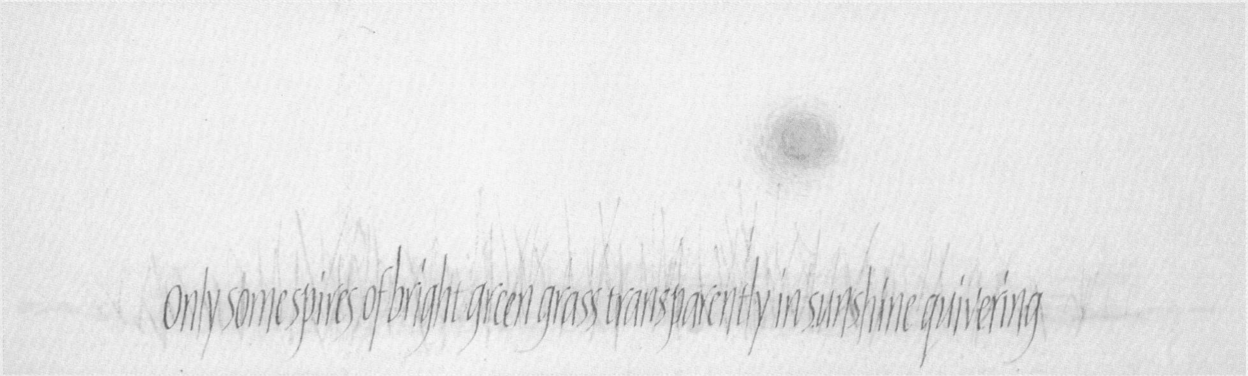

Only some spires of bright green grass transparently in sunshine quivering

Lindsay Castell, UK
ONLY SOME SPIRES (Emily Brontë)

90 × 280mm (3½ × 11in)

Gouache and watercolour on Wookey hole paper, using
a metal nib and a brush.

GALLERY

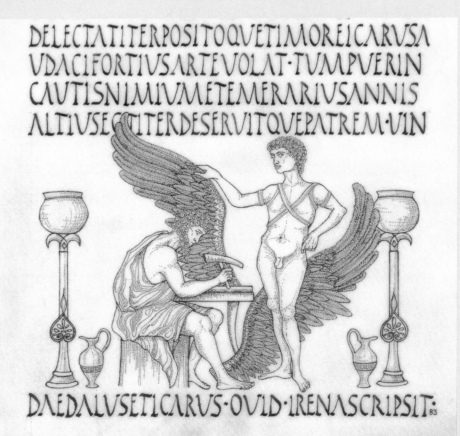

Peter Halliday, UK
SIR GAWAYNE AND THE
GRENE KNIGHT

445 × 375mm (17½ × 15in)

Gouache on Canson paper,
written with metal nibs.

Irena Armstrong, UK
ICARUS

178 × 533mm (7 × 21in)

Untreated stretched calf vellum.
Rustic capitals in brown ink, using
a metal nib. Illustration taken
from a Roman base relief and
done with a technical drawing pen.

18

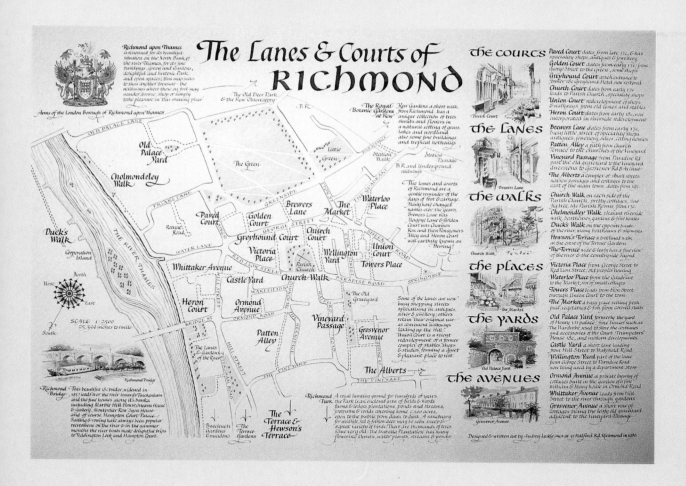

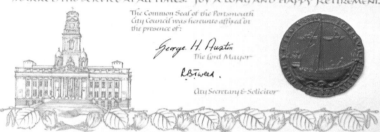

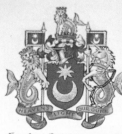

Audrey Leckie, UK

THE LANES AND COURTS OF RICHMOND

47 × 63cm (18½ × 25in)

Chinese ink and watercolours
written with metal nibs on
machine-made paper. Designed
for reproduction at a size of
28 × 40cm (11 × 16in).

David John Graham, UK

PRESENTATION SCROLL (John Haslegrave)

355 × 367mm (14 × 14½in)

Watercolour and gold on vellum.

19

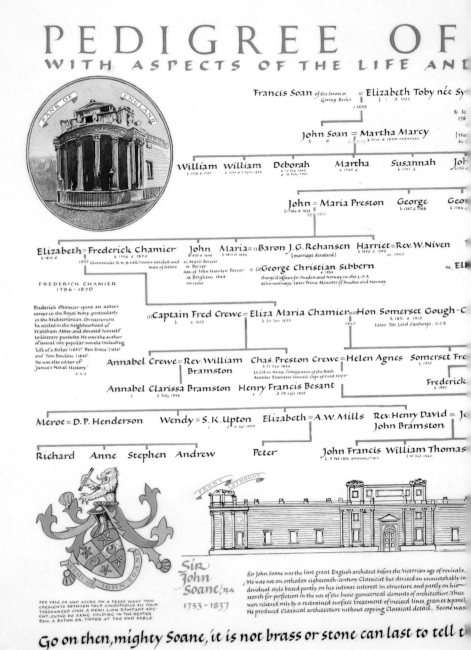

Gerald Fleuss, UK
PEDIGREE OF SOAN OF GORING

76 × 51cm (30 × 20in)

Stretch-mounted vellum with Chinese ink, gouache, shell gold and gold leaf on PVA. Quill and steel pens of various sizes. The pedigree commences with Francis Soan of the Swan Inn, Goring, Berks whose grandson was Sir John Soane, the eminent 18th century architect. The research for the decorative elements was done mostly at the Sir John Soane Museum, London.
(By kind permission of Mrs Patricia Robinson)

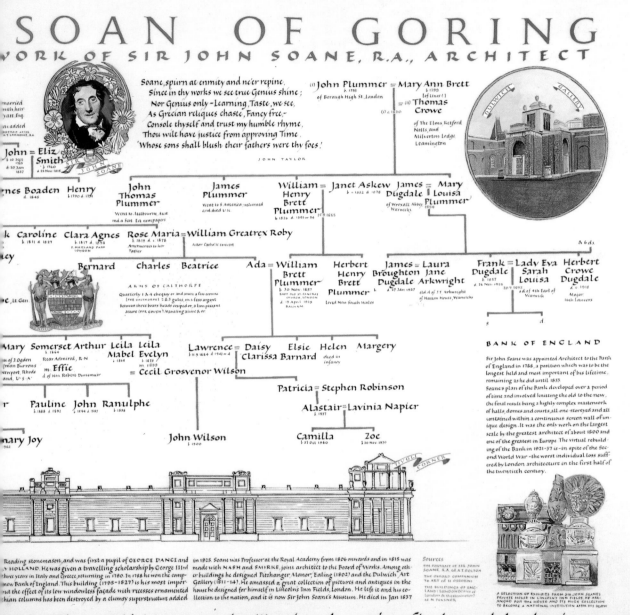

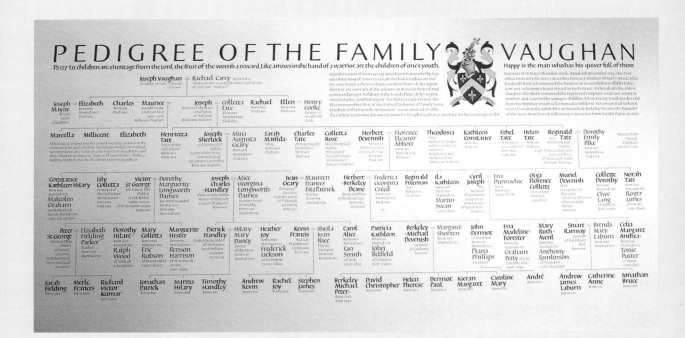

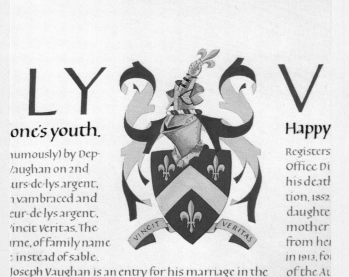

Richard Middleton, UK

VAUGHAN FAMILY TREE

56 × 117cm (22 × 46in)

Gouache on Saunders Antiquarian paper, written with metal nibs. The title and heraldry were painted with a sable brush. *(By kind permission of the Revd. Patrick Vaughan)*

Nick Stewart, UK

"REEDS"

77 × 305mm (31/3 × 12in)

The background "Reeds" on this packaging was written with an automatic pen and then transferred to a screen and printed as a repeat gradation on to black paper. A single screen print of "Reeds" was then made in a brighter colour.

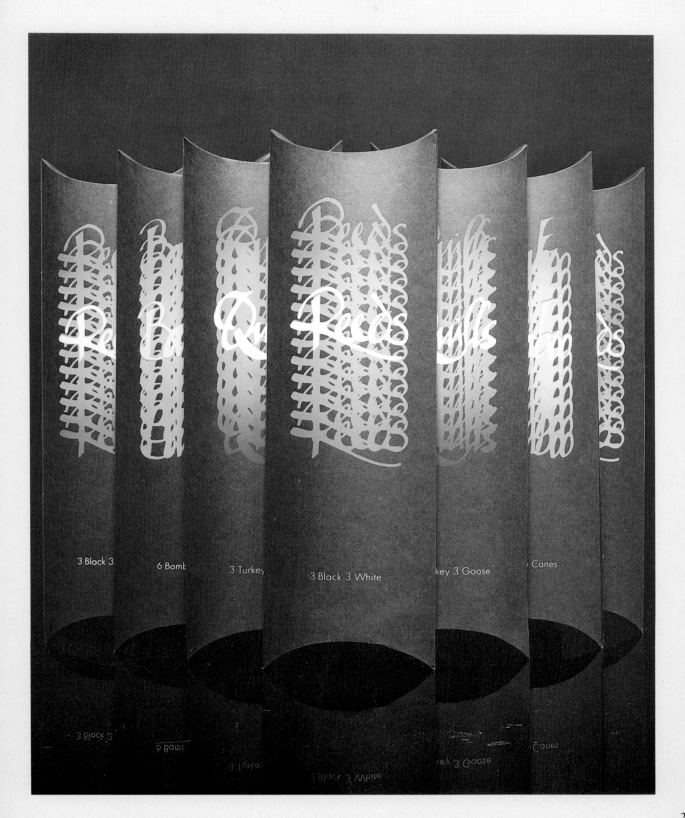

3 Black 3   6 Bamb   3 Turkey   3 Black 3 White   key 3 Goose   Canes

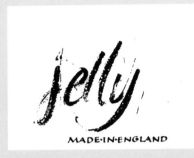

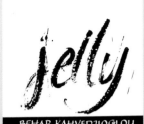

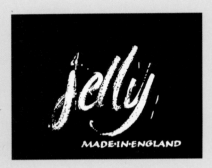

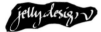

9. HEATHMANS ROAD
PARSONS GREEN
LONDON · SW6 4TJ
01 736 9036 (5 LINES)

Lilly Lee, UK

JELLY

Corporate logo for fashion designer, originally rapidly drawn with Chinese brush on to textured paper, then reduced. Small letters written with metal nibs. Printed black on white, white on black, and white on grey.

9. HEATHMANS ROAD
PARSONS GREEN
LONDON · SW6 4TJ
01 736 9036 (5 LINES)

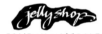

70 NEW KINGS ROAD
FULHAM LONDON SW6 4LS
TELEPHONE 01 736 2548

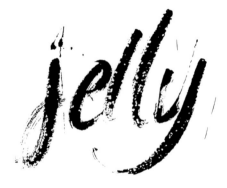

With Compliments

Lilly Lee, UK

PHIL REYNOLDS

Corporate logo for costume designer, written with pen and ink, and printed thermographically.

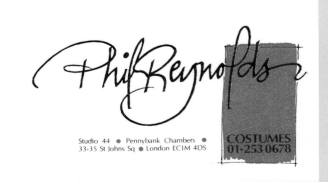

Studio 44 ● Pennybank Chambers ●
33-35 St Johns Sq ● London EC1M 4DS

COSTUMES
01-253 0678

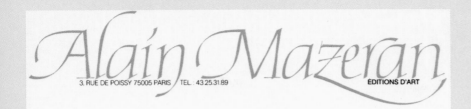

3, RUE DE POISSY 75005 PARIS / TEL : 43.25.31.89   ÉDITIONS D'ART

Jean Larcher, France
ALAIN MAZERAN

Corporate logo for art publisher, written with pen and ink, printed on Conqueror paper by offset lithography.

PERSONAL LOGO

Watercolour and inks written with an automatic pen on Bristol paper. Printed in full colour by offset lithography.

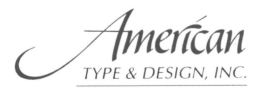

TÉLEX 250.303 + – R.C. A 308930064 PARIS

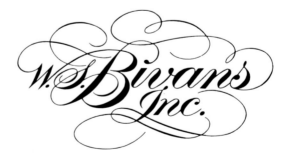

Robert Boyajian, USA
AMERICAN TYPE & DESIGN INC

Pen and ink logo for stationery set.
(Art director: Eileen Kirban)

W.S. BIVANS INC

Pen and ink logo for stationery set, printed thermographically.

25

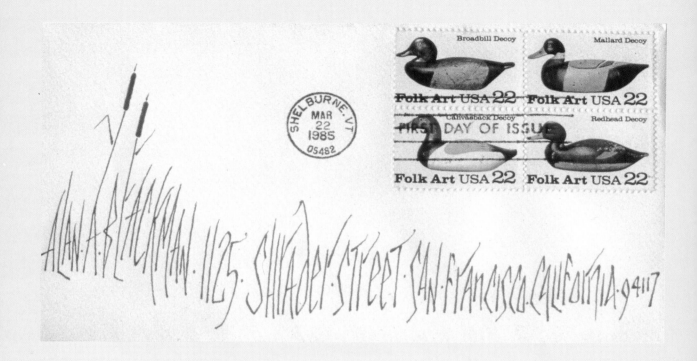

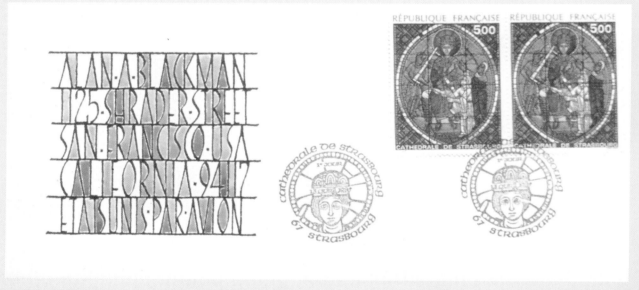

Alan Blackman, USA
LETTERS TO MYSELF

19 × 10cm (7½ × 4in)

Two envelopes from a set of 750 first-day covers, calligraphically addressed in designs which reflect or complement the stamps. The colours are ground from Chinese stick ink and mixed with gum arabic to prevent the letters from smudging. Lettering done with turkey quills, and a fine pointed steel "copperplate" pen.

Alan Blackman, USA
DECORATIVE ALPHABET

51 × 66cm (20 × 26in)

Fluorescent water-based paints applied with turkey quills on black Japanese mokiki paper. Some colours required several coats of paint.

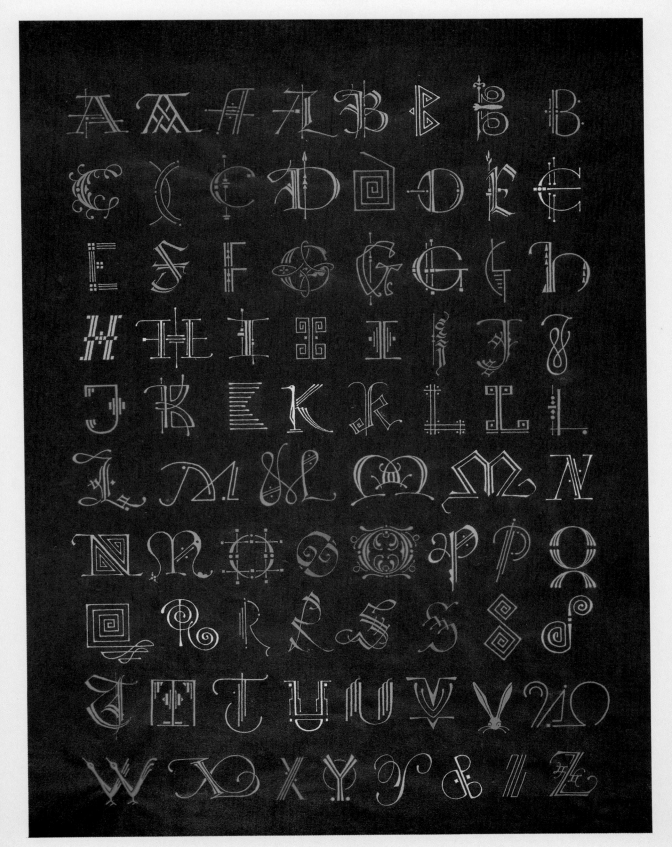

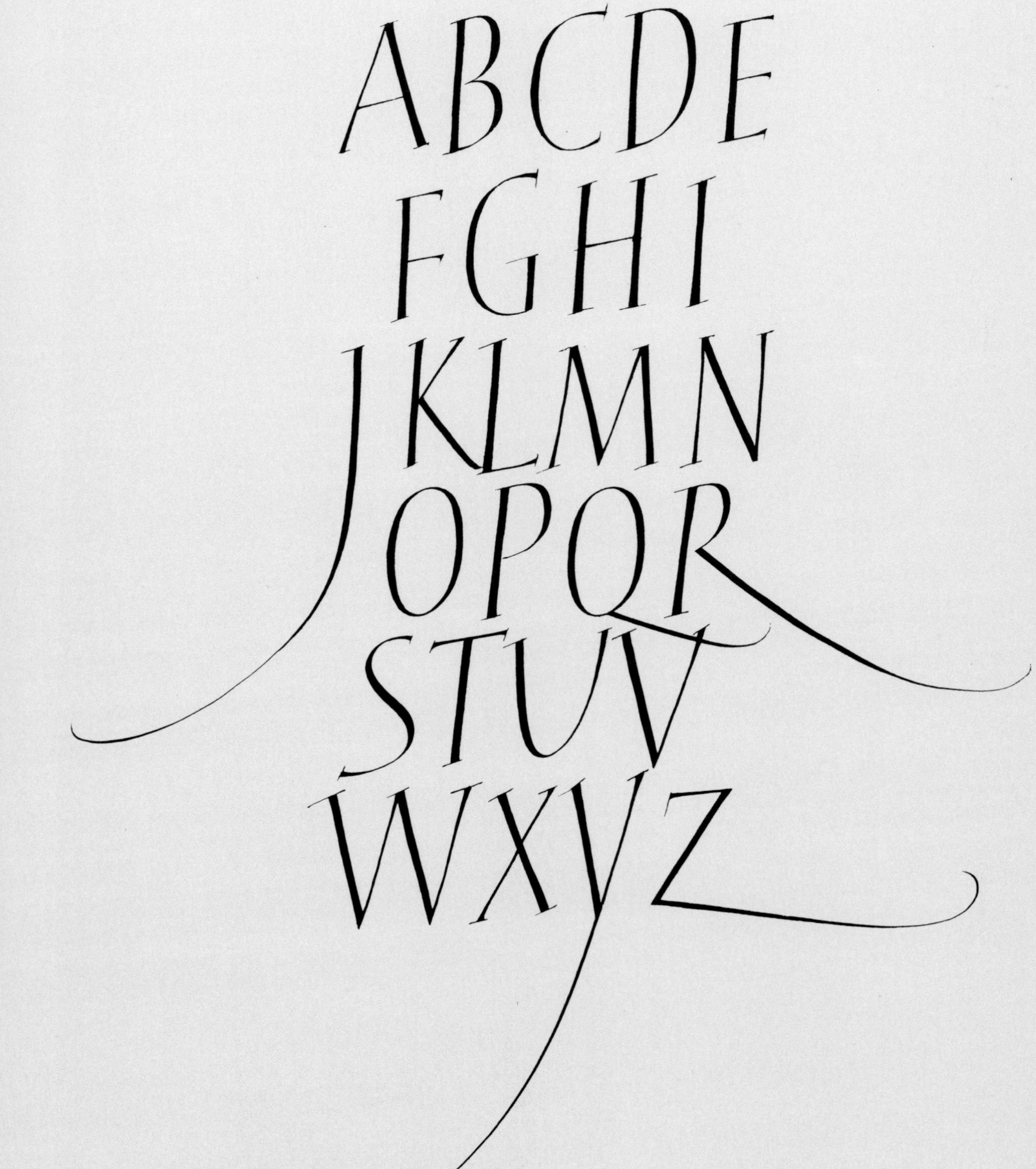

ABCDE
FGHI
JKLMN
OPQR
STUV
WXYZ

Gaynor Goffe, UK
VERSAL ALPHABET

51 × 38cm (20 × 15in)
Pen and ink, prepared for reproduction.

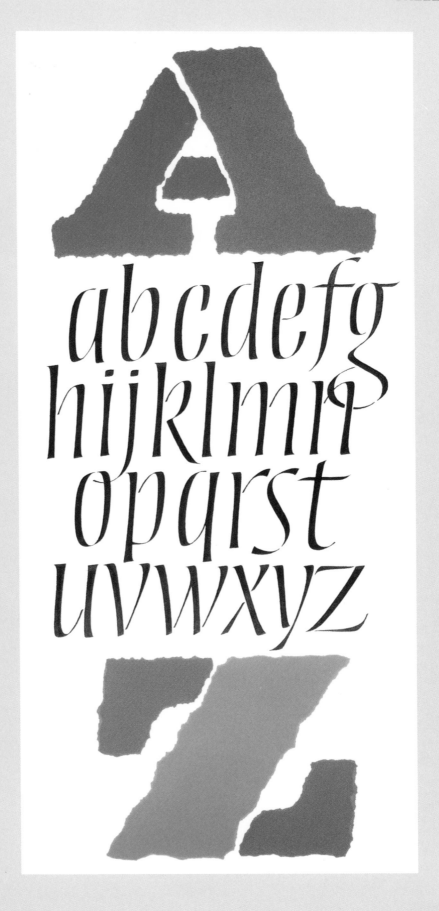

Michael Harvey, UK

ALPHABET

74 × 33cm (29 × 13in)

Torn paper initials, pen drawn alphabet.

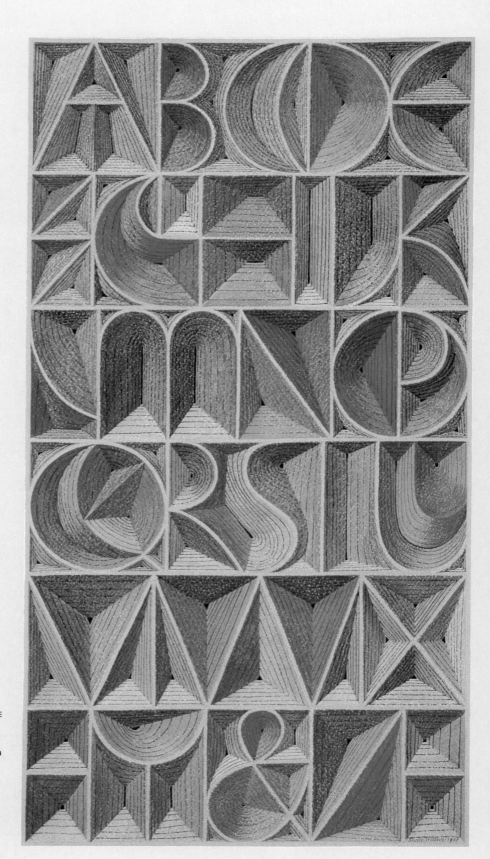

Sheila Waters, USA

ALPHABET IN THREE DIMENSIONS, ONE

46 × 24cm (18 × 9½in)

One of two paintings, executed in gouache and oil pastel, which explore the three-dimensional possibilities of the alphabet structure while confining the colour scheme to the magenta/blue quadrant of the spectrum.

FOR NOTHING
WORTHY PROVING
CAN BE PROVEN,
NOR YET DISPROVEN·
WHEREFORE THOU
BE WISE, CLEAVE
EVER TO THE SUNN-
IER SIDE OF DOUBT·

David H. Nicholls, UK
THE ANCIENT SAGE (Tennyson)

160 × 120mm (6¼ × 4¾in)

Brush-drawn letters, gouache on
MBM Arches paper. The letter
forms and their arrangement
were based on those found in the
12th century 'Bodleian bible'; the
freedom of form being used to fit
the text into a definite area.

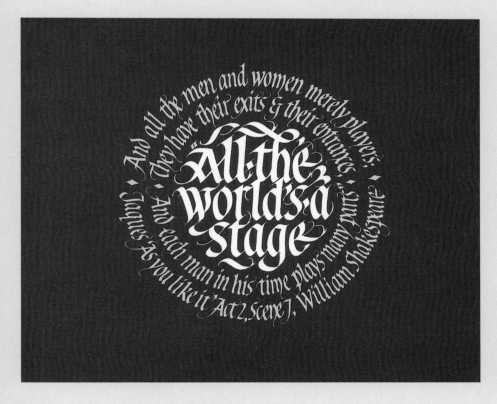

Ieuan Rees, UK
GREETINGS CARD

152 × 123mm (6 × 4¾in)

Two-colour printing on white
paper.

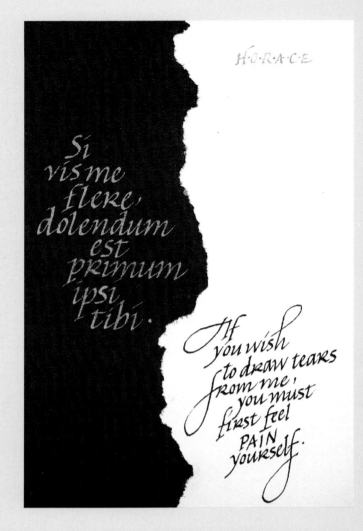

Margaret Prasthofer, USA

HORACE

152 × 100mm (6 × 4in)

Stick ink and shell gold on
handmade paper.

Caroline Carmichael, UK

YOU ENGLISH WORDS (Edward Thomas)

10 × 10cm (4 × 4in) closed
61 × 11cm (24 × 4¼in) open

Concertina-fold manuscript written with metal nibs in two
shades of grey gouache on grey Fabriano paper.

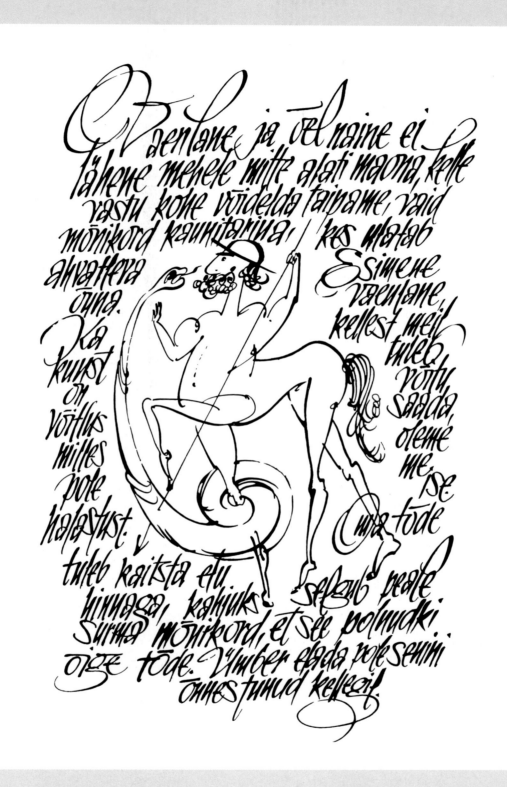

Villu Toots, USSR

QUOTATION

315 × 195mm (12½ × 7½in)

Drawing and writing in pen and ink.

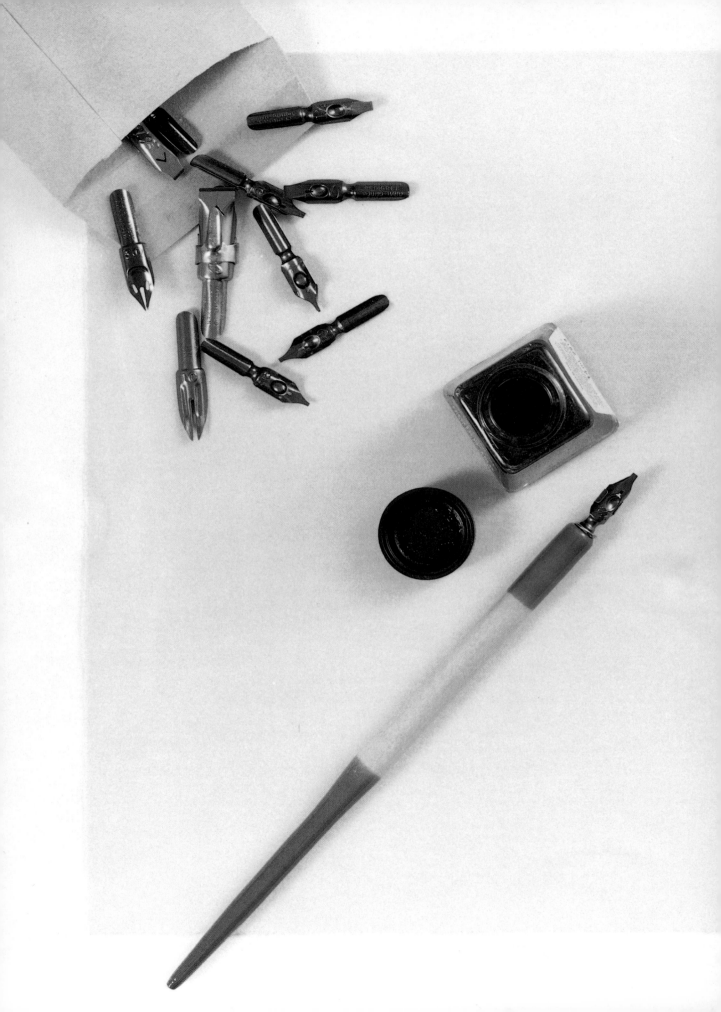

Materials + Penmanship

This information-packed reference section sets out clearly the equipment you will need for the projects in the book, and also goes into details about optional additions. You are then taken through a carefully planned introduction to writing with a broad-edged pen, arranging your work space, and learning a method for studying scripts. This is followed by a series of exemplars for seven writing styles. Basic design principles, preparing work for the printers, and practical tips on general working methods prepare you for the main section of the book.

Equipment

When you first start, pen, paper and ink are the only absolutely essential items you will need, however you will probably soon want to build up your supplies. The illustration shows a selection of the materials that will be useful for the projects in the book.

Take good care of your materials: when you have finished working, wipe the ink off the pen nib with a rag or tissue; ideally, you should remove the reservoir and the nib, wash them, and then dry thoroughly (do not let the metal housing of a pen get wet); brushes should be cleaned and stored in a jar with hair uppermost; paper should be stored flat, or loosely rolled; lids and caps of inks and paints should be replaced after use; protect knife blades by embedding them in a cork when not in use.

Basic equipment 1 Drawing board; **2** scissors; **3** craft knife or **4** scalpel; **5** set-square; **6** pencils; **7** eraser; **8** ruler; **9** T-square; **10** masking tape (for fixing paper to the board when ruling up); **11** layout paper (at least A3 size – 420 × 297mm (16½ × 11¾in); **12** stick glue, or **13** rubber cement and **14** plastic spreader; **15** fountain pens, **16** broad-edged felt pens, **17** carpenters pencils

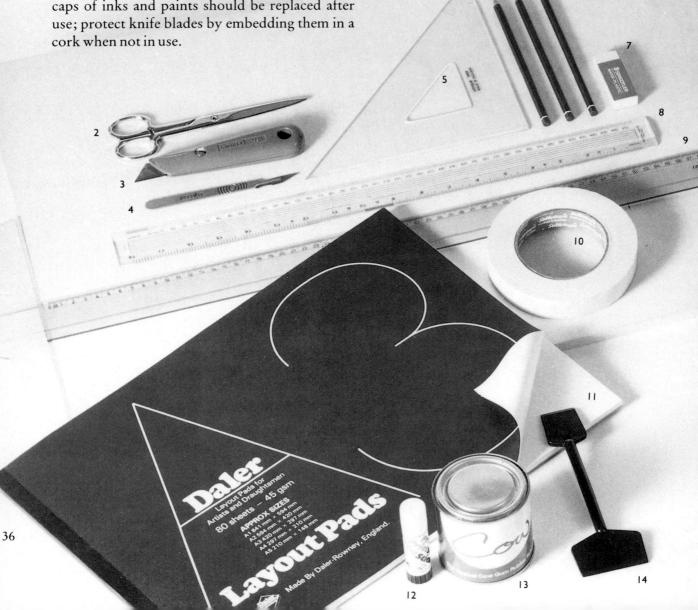

and **18** automatic pens are useful writing tools; **19** pen holders and **20** nibs and reservoirs were used for the projects in the book; **21** non-waterproof black ink; **22** coloured ink; **23** palette; **24** gouache (water-based opaque paint) or **25** watercolours; **26** brushes (chisel-edged for writing, cheap synthetic brush for loading paint on to pen, fine sable brushes for painting). You will also need a supply of other papers, such as tracing paper and cartridge paper; a water jar and rag or tissues.

Additional equipment These will be useful additions to your list: **a** Metal rule (when cutting paper with a knife); **b** technical drawing pen (for ruling accurate, unvaried lines); **c** ruling pen (with adjustable blades which can be set to various widths and loaded with paint to rule even lines); **d** dividers (for marking out ruling widths); **e** compasses; **f** bone folder (for smoothing down paper folds); **g** masking fluid (a rubber fluid used as a resist); **h** gum arabic and **i** ox gall (optional additives to paint); **j** sketchbook.

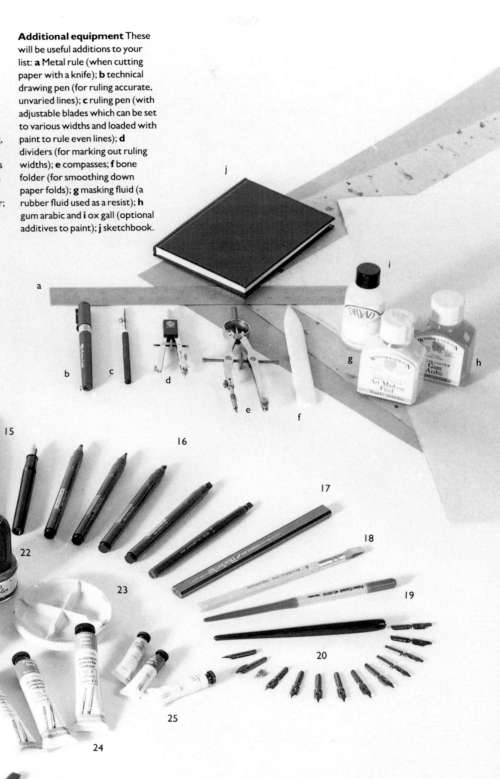

PENS, PENCILS AND BRUSHES

ALL THE pen lettering for the projects was written with dip pens – metal nibs held in a pen holder. Once mastered, they are convenient to use, and will give consistent results. There is, however, a huge variety of writing tools on the market, and new products are always being developed, so it pays to make regular visits to art shops. Pens can also be made by hand – the reed and the quill pen are the traditional tools of the calligrapher.

DIP PENS

Pen holders vary in diameter, profile, length and weight. A round barrel tends to be more comfortable to hold than one that is angled. Avoid pen holders with attached reservoirs as they allow little control over the ink flow.

Broad-edged nibs are cut square, or at an angle (right oblique for right-handers, left oblique for left-handers). The size range varies according to the manufacturer. The nibs used in the projects are: Rexel/Mitchell nibs (sized range from 0.6mm to 3.3mm, numbered from 6 to 0) and Brause nibs (sized in millimetres from ½mm to 5mm). Brause nibs have a right-oblique angle, are made of a more resilient metal, and the reservoir is attached to the top of the nib; Mitchell nibs can have a reservoir attached to the underside; Speedball nibs are another popular brand which come in several ranges. New nibs have a

protective coating of lacquer which should be removed before use by washing in hot water, or by holding the nib over a lighted match for a couple of seconds, and then running cold water over the nib.

Pens with broad nibs that are fixed into the holder, such as automatic pens (*see p37*) and coit pens, may be easier for beginners to use at first. These are available in large sizes, and with

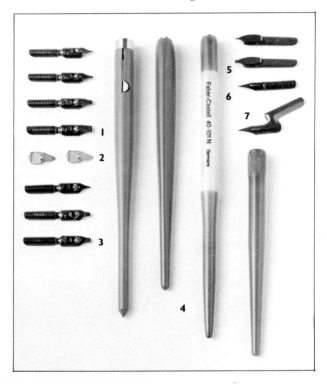

1 Mitchell square-cut, "round hand" nibs for right-handed calligraphers; 2 reservoirs; 3 left-oblique nibs for left-handed calligraphers; 4 a variety of pen holders; 5 Brause nibs; 6 flexible, pointed drawing pen (Gillot 404) and 7 elbow nib used for copperplate writing.

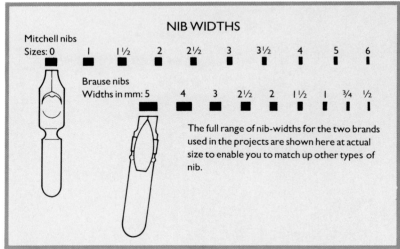

NIB WIDTHS

Mitchell nibs
Sizes: 0   1   1½   2   2½   3   3½   4   5   6

Brause nibs
Widths in mm: 5   4   3   2½   2   1½   1   ¾   ½

The full range of nib-widths for the two brands used in the projects are shown here at actual size to enable you to match up other types of nib.

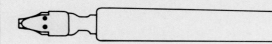
double-pointed ends for a decorative effect.

Flexible, pointed nibs are used for copperplate writing. Elbow nibs are specially designed for this purpose, but more successful results can be achieved with a pointed drawing pen.

FOUNTAIN PENS AND FELT PENS

Fountain pens with broad-edged nibs are easy to use, but, in general, they do not offer the size-range, or the sharpness of dip pens. Always use fountain pen ink.

The fluidity of felt pens allows a freedom and spontaneity that makes them invaluable for working on roughs. However, they cannot give a sharp line, they have a relatively short life, and the ink is generally not permanent.

PENCILS

You will need two or three different grades of pencil—an HB pencil if you intend to erase ruling lines, and a harder pencil (say a 2H) for lines you intend to leave. Two pencils can be taped together to give a double-pointed "square-edged" writing tool which is very useful when learning the principle of the edged pen (*see pp44-5 and p117*). Carpenters pencils are particularly suitable as they have a broad, flat lead which can be sharpened with a knife to an edge.

BRUSHES

Sable hair (which comes from the tail of the kolinsky, or Siberian weasel) is best for pointed and chisel-edged lettering brushes as it keeps its shape and makes a fine line. However, some chisel-edged synthetic brushes are extremely good, and they are less expensive. If you are a left-hander having trouble with metal nibs, try using a chisel-edged brush.

CUTTING A PEN

A "rural pen", cut from a reed or a piece of bamboo is fun to make and use, and may encourage you to investigate the finer art of quill cutting. You will need a piece of bamboo (a fresh piece will be easier to cut), a fretsaw, and a craft knife with a fixed blade.

1 With a fretsaw cut a piece of bamboo about 20cm (8in) long. Make sure you cut well away from the nodes.

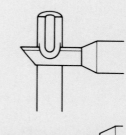

2 Use a craft knife to shape the nib. The first cut is a diagonal slice off the end. Cut away from your body. Make several cuts and remove some of the thickness of the bamboo from the inside of the stem.

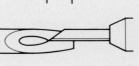

3 Place the outside of the long side of the nib on a cutting surface and make a central slit.

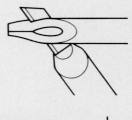

4 Make a scooped cut along one side to determine the width of the nib. Cut the other side of the nib, starting at the same level.

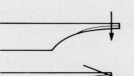

5 Cut the end off the pen for a square or angled nib.

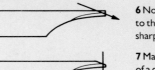

6 Now cut a beveled edge to the top of the nib to sharpen it.

7 Make a final vertical sliver of a cut to trim the end. Before using the pen, soak it first in ink as it will be very absorbent.

Paints and Inks

It is important to find an ink that suits you and that you can rely on. This can be more difficult than it sounds – not only do brands vary in their composition, but they also tend to vary from batch to batch. In addition, the quality of an ink cannot be considered in isolation – much depends on the paper, the slope of the writing surface, the type and size of the nib, and the position of the reservoir. Inks should be judged mainly for their flow and density, and this can only be discovered by trial and error. Permanence, another important factor, will only be revealed in time. Non-waterproof black ink is generally recommended, but try others, and also consider using black gouache as an alternative to black ink.

Gouache and watercolour are the paints most commonly used by calligraphers. The popularity of coloured inks has recently been increased by the introduction of improved products. It is also worth experimenting with other media, such as acrylics and fabric dyes, which are not traditionally associated with calligraphy. Powdered pigments can be bought and mixed with a binder, such as gum arabic, to make your own paints. For the beginner, however, the most reliable results can be achieved with gouache paint, which gives a strong, opaque covering.

INKS

Always shake the bottle before using ink. It can be loaded into the pen by dipping, or by using a dipper or a brush to fill the underside of the nib. If the nib is dipped, shake any excess ink back into the bottle and wipe the top of the nib, so that the ink does not flood when you start using the pen.

Non-waterproof black ink is the most suitable black ink for the calligrapher, and has been used for most of the projects done in black ink. Brands vary in quality, but a good non-waterproof ink will give a fine line. If necessary, the ink can be thinned by adding a little distilled water.

Waterproof black ink is not recommended for calligraphy as it clogs up the pen and does not produce fine hairline strokes. If your writing has to be waterproof, wipe the nib frequently while working.

Many coloured drawing inks are unsuitable for calligraphy - they produce inconsistent lines, they clog up in the pen, and, being coloured with dyes, rather than pigments, they are not permanent. Coloured writing inks, however, vary greatly in quality. There are some versatile, new pigmented inks which can be mixed with a medium to alter consistency.

Inks and paints Gradually build
up a selection of inks and paints,
so that when you start a piece of
work you are not restricted by
lack of choice.

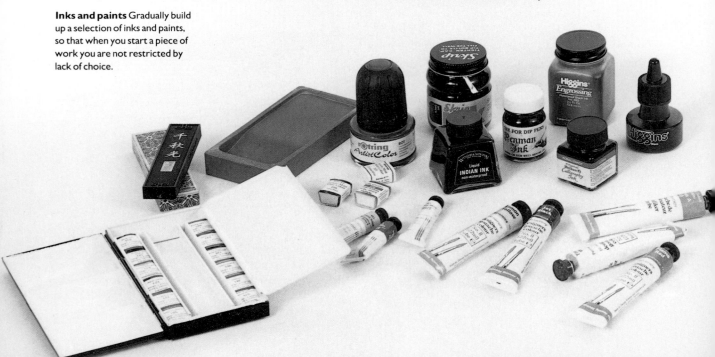

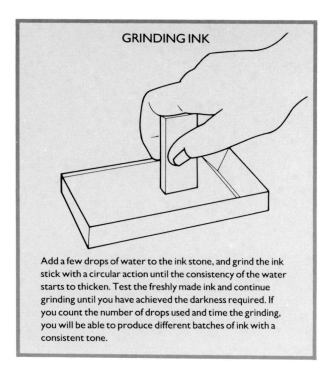

GRINDING INK

Add a few drops of water to the ink stone, and grind the ink stick with a circular action until the consistency of the water starts to thicken. Test the freshly made ink and continue grinding until you have achieved the darkness required. If you count the number of drops used and time the grinding, you will be able to produce different batches of ink with a consistent tone.

Fountain pen ink is specially designed to give the correct flow for these pens, although some brands also work well with dip pens.

By grinding your own ink you can control the density of the tone. You will need a Chinese ink stick, an ink stone and some distilled water, preferably in a dropper bottle.

PAINTS

Gouache is also known as "designer's colour". An opaque water-based paint which is available in a wide range of colours, it can produce a consistent, flat, opaque line when used with a pen, and will also give flat broad areas of colour when applied with a brush.

Most brands have different series, of varying permanence. Buy the most permanent colour you can afford, or it will fade. Start with a basic set – zinc white, ivory black, cobalt blue, flame red, lemon yellow, oxide of chromium – and add to it gradually.

Watercolour is manufactured in tubes, cakes and pans. Pans have the least additives, but tubes are more convenient to use. The more expensive "artist's" colours are of a higher quality and are more permanent. Watercolour gives a delicate, translucent colour, and it is essential to use clean water for colour mixing, or the freshness of the medium is lost. Chinese white can be added to watercolour to make it opaque.

When mixing paint from a tube, use a small container, or a palette with small wells. Squeeze out a small quantity of paint, add drops of clean, preferably distilled, water with a brush, and mix until the paint reaches the consistency of single cream and will drop off the brush. Add water gradually – remember that you can thin a paint much more easily than you can thicken it. Always replace the lids of tube colour, otherwise they will dry out, and the paint will go hard.

Colours should be mixed gradually, starting with the lightest colour and adding to it. Ideally, you should have different brushes for each colour, and change the water frequently to avoid muddiness in mixing. Mixing tube colours 24 hours before you intend to use them will improve them as it gives the glycerine a chance to evaporate. Keep a record of the colour mixes and the proportions used. When working on a finished piece, be sure to mix up enough of each colour to complete the job.

When using paint in a pen, you can improve its flow by lowering the drawing board to a shallower angle than when working with ink. It also helps to work without a reservoir. Use a brush to load the pen with paint. Stir the paint frequently to stop it separating, and clean the nib from time to time to prevent the paint from drying on it. You may have to add a drop of water to the paint as it evaporates.

If you have trouble in getting the paint to flow, try adding a drop of gum arabic or ox gall. Gum arabic increases the fluidity and the gloss of the paint, and also increases its adherence to the paper surface; ox gall will improve the adhesive quality of the paint. Both gum arabic and ox gall should be added one drop at a time, from the end of a matchstick, rather than the end of a paintbrush (particularly since ox gall is very bitter).

PAPER

Your choice of writing surface will have an important effect on the character and quality of your work. Most art stores stock a fairly limited range, so it is worth visiting a specialist paper shop to discover the possibilities available to you. You can also try a number of other surfaces: fabric is an interesting alternative for brush lettering, and vellum (calfskin) has an extremely responsive surface (it generally needs a certain amount of preparation).

It is useful to know some facts about paper as it can make your choice easier, although in the end the only real proof of the suitability of a paper is the results you get from actually putting pen to paper, and your own subjective reaction to how it looks and feels. Find a paper that you can rely on for everyday use (layout paper is used for much of the work in the projects), but keep an open mind about trying others.

Paper is made from vegetable fibres which have been separated, suspended in water and beaten (cotton fibres produce the best quality paper); machine made paper is formed on a continuous roller, handmade paper is formed between a deckle and mould (two sides of a flat sieve-like mesh); it is then dried and pressed.

Machine made paper is generally less expensive; its quality is consistent, and the sheets are cut with regular edges (which is useful when ruling up). It is often available in a large range of colours.

Handmade paper offers a wider variety in weight and surface, and particularly in character.

It is formed in separate sheets and has four "deckle" edges. It can be quite expensive, but high quality handmade paper does allow for mistakes to be erased.

Mouldmade paper is machine made paper which imitates handmade paper, and is made in sheets, rather than on a continuous roll. It has two deckle edges and two torn edges.

SURFACE AND TEXTURE

The surface of a paper should be selected for its suitability for the work, its compatability with the pen and ink, and with the scale of the writing. The idea of a "right" and "wrong" side of a paper is misleading – use any side you please.

The surface of a paper depends mainly on the fibres used in making it, the type of mesh in the deckle and mould, and on the way it is pressed when dried: *Laid paper* has the pattern of the horizontal and vertical lines from the deckle and mould impressed on the paper; *wove paper* has a more even texture which results from the deckle and mould having a woven mesh. *Hot pressed* (or HP) has the smoothest finish. The paper is pressed between metal sheets or rollers (either hot or cold). Generally regarded as the most suitable pressing for calligraphy paper. *Not pressed* (or Not) has been lightly pressed. It has a slightly textured surface, or "tooth". *Rough* has been allowed to dry naturally, with no pressing involved. Its rugged texture makes it suitable only for use with a very broad writing tool, particularly a brush.

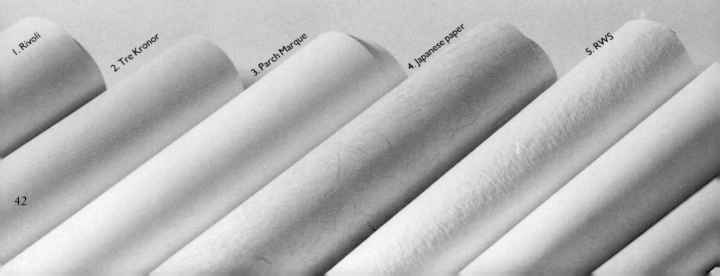

1. Rivoli   2. Tre Kronor   3. Parch Marque   4. Japanese paper   5. RWS

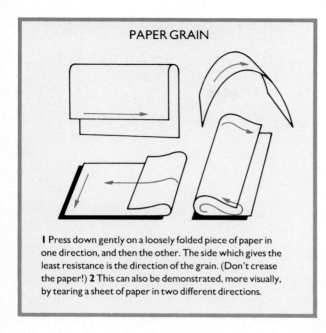

PAPER GRAIN

1 Press down gently on a loosely folded piece of paper in one direction, and then the other. The side which gives the least resistance is the direction of the grain. (Don't crease the paper!) **2** This can also be demonstrated, more visually, by tearing a sheet of paper in two different directions.

SIZING, WEIGHT AND GRAIN

The absorbency of a paper is determined by the way it has been treated with size (glue). An un-sized paper (e.g. blotting paper) allows the ink to spread through the fibres; a highly sized paper will repel the ink.

The weight of paper is measured in pounds per ream (i.e. 500 sheets of a particular size) or in grams per square metre (gsm). Paper is made to several different ranges of standard sizes.

Paper weight should be carefully considered, particularly for a manuscript book, when you will have to think of the bulk of the folded sheets. Paper weight also affects the degree of "show-through" (i.e. how much of the writing can be seen on the opposite side of the paper).

Machine made paper has a grain produced during the manufacturing process. The paper will fold and tear more easily in this direction. Handmade paper has no grain.

It is important to establish the grain direction of a paper if it is to be folded for a greetings card, or a manuscript book, otherwise the paper will not open or fall correctly. The direction can be detected by tearing or folding.

RECOMMENDED PAPERS

Keep a good stock of useful basic papers, and also some better, more interesting papers. Layout paper is useful for roughs, and for finished work that will be printed. It has a good "tooth" for an edged pen; and is thin, yet strong. Use board or cartridge paper to paste-up on. When using cartridge paper for writing with dip pens, make sure it is of good quality. Tracing paper is handy for refining lettering, layouts and designs. Crystal parchment (or glassine) is a thin release paper, used for protecting work, and sometimes when burnishing gold. Brown wrapping paper (kraft paper) has a surprisingly good writing surface, is economical, and has ready-ruled lines.

STORAGE AND HANDLING

Paper should be stored flat if possible, or rolled up very loosely. It should not be kept in damp conditions, nor in very hot or cold conditions. Always handle with care, holding the paper with both (clean) hands in a loose curve; it is very difficult to remove small creases.

1 Large strong sheet; **2** pronounced rib, wide colour range; **3** mock parchment; **4** decorative papers, use with brush or reed; **5** handmade watercolour paper; **6** popular handmade calligraphy paper; **7** and **8** several brands, wide colour range, flecked; **9** smooth surface, cream colour; **10** bright white, large range of weights, size and surface; **11** watercolour paper.

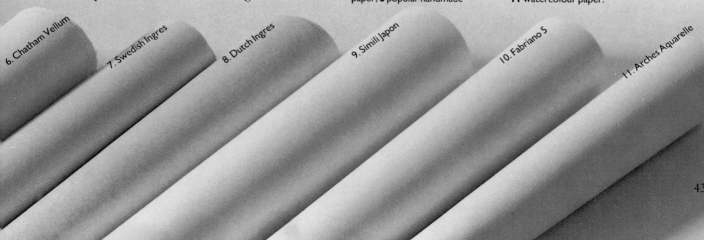

6. Chatham Vellum   7. Swedish Ingres   8. Dutch Ingres   9. Simili Japon   10. Fabriano 5   11. Arches Aquarelle

Starting Out

Before even thinking about letters, take some time to get to know the pens you are using, and how they work. The characteristic calligraphic contrast of thick and thin strokes is achieved by holding a broad-edged pen at a constant angle. However, for copperplate writing a pointed, flexible pen is used, which needs a very different approach (*see p62*).

The idea of holding a broad-edged pen at a particular angle is easily grasped by some people, while others take a long time to get the hang of it. To make it easier at the beginning, it is a good idea to start with a wide, simple pen - broad-edged felt pens, or automatic pens are ideal. Alternatively, try improvising by cutting a piece of thin balsa wood, or a lollipop stick, with a straight edge, or cut yourself a bamboo pen. The important thing is that you should not be inhibited by the pen you are using.

So, with "pen" in hand, dip it in ink and start to experiment. Using cheap paper should encourage you to cover as much paper as possible. You will soon discover for yourself the different effects made by the pen when held at different angles.

As soon as you feel comfortable with your pen, take a large piece of layout or cartridge paper, and rule some horizontal pencil lines across it (approximately 5cm/2in apart if your pen is about 12mm/½in wide, or 2cm/¾in apart for a pen of 5mm/¼in). Start with some simple strokes and geometric forms (*illustrations 1, 2 and 3*), concentrating first on how to handle the pen – the idea of pen angle, the order and direction of strokes, hand and arm movement; then move on to consider basic form and variety of weight.

PEN ANGLE

This is the first important aspect to understand when writing with a broad-edged pen. It actually refers to the angle that is made between the edge of the pen nib and the writing line. It has nothing to do with the steepness of the angle between the pen holder and the board (*see pp46-7*).

THE ORDER OF STROKES

Start with the square in illustration 3. The order of strokes (i.e. from top to bottom, and from left to right) sets the pattern for writing letters. In general, broad pen strokes are pulled towards you, rather than pushed.

The pen will start more easily on a thin line (this is particularly true of a dip pen, and is not so obvious with a coarser pen), so make a habit of moving into broad straight strokes from a thin lead-in line. A curve must start on a thin line; its position is determined by the pen angle, and circles should be written with two strokes, to avoid pushing the pen.

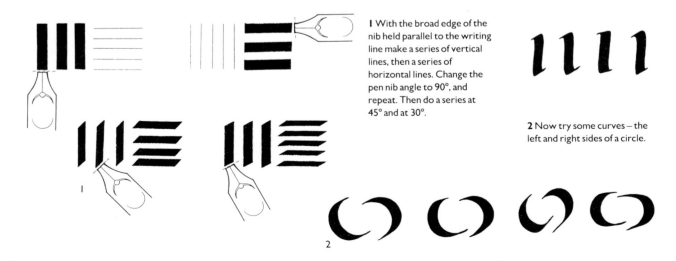

1 With the broad edge of the nib held parallel to the writing line make a series of vertical lines, then a series of horizontal lines. Change the pen nib angle to 90°, and repeat. Then do a series at 45° and at 30°.

2 Now try some curves – the left and right sides of a circle.

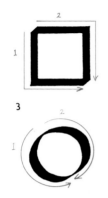

3 Draw a square and a circle with the nib at 45° to the writing line as shown.

4 Draw a series of squares, starting with the pen at 0°, and then at increasingly steeper angles. Notice how the change in pen angle affects basic form.

5 Now make a series of circles in a similar way.

Hand and arm movement should be positive, but relaxed. Allow your whole arm to move for more freedom in writing very long strokes, rather than cramping up your fingers.

BASIC FORM AND WEIGHT

When you write with the broad-edged pen, you are actually adding weight to an underlying skeletal shape. It is the strength of these "bones" that is of prime importance to letter forms. To see this more clearly (*illustration 7*), draw a circle with one pencil and then trace over it with the double pencils, keeping the same point on the circle for both strokes. The weighted circle now appears as two overlapping circles. Shade in the enclosed area.

By using the same nib (*illustration 8*), but increasing or decreasing the height of the shapes, you will start to understand what is meant by "weight" (the relation of the nib width to the height of the form or letter). Variety in weight can also be achieved by writing at a constant height, but changing the width of the nib.

6 Writing diagonals at different angles will make you think more about the direction of the strokes. Broad strokes are more easily pulled than pushed, but the thinnest "hair line" strokes are written easily in either direction.

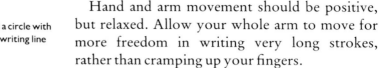

Pen patterns Before going into the complexities of letter forms, try some pattern-making to familiarize yourself with different tools and materials and to gain confidence in using them. It is important to feel that you can always return to basics, and also to enjoy the shapes that the pen can make.

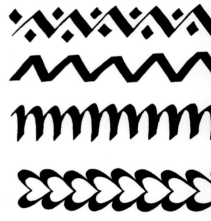

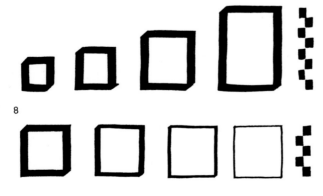

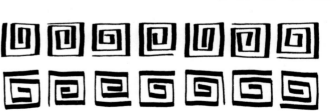

PREPARING TO WRITE

Having loosened up and familiarized yourself with the characteristics of the broad-edged pen, you will be ready to concentrate on the letters themselves. For this you will have to be more precise about the way you work, which means thinking about your working environment, your posture, the angle of the board, how to hold the pen, and how to prepare your paper with accurately ruled lines. This may sound daunting, but in fact it will soon become second nature. Getting the basics right at the start will enable you to produce better results in the long-term. However, the most important factor is to be relaxed – an agitated mind will not allow the hand to produce good letters.

It is very important to have a chair and table at the correct height, so that you can sit up straight to work. An uncomfortable position will not only give you back strain, but will also hinder your lettering. Set up your board in a good general light. If you are working with colour, make sure you work in daylight, as colour values are drastically affected by artificial light. Set the board at a comfortable angle, but bear in mind that the angle affects the ink flow: it should be about 45° when writing with ink, lower when writing with a very broad pen, or when using paint. Prop it up on a sturdy object, or an easel. An adjustable drawing board with a parallel motion is better still.

Pad the surface of the board with several sheets of blotting paper, or cartridge paper, for a more responsive writing surface. Your paper should not be taped down while you write. If you are using paper from a pad, remove the sheets and use them singly. It is also a good idea to tape a second sheet of paper to the lower part of the board, as this will protect the paper you are writing on from the grease of your hand, give you somewhere to rest both hands, and also act as a writing-line guide.

Pen angle is discussed on the previous page, in relation to the angle between the nib and the writing line. Another factor to consider is the angle of the pen holder in relation to the writing surface. Again, this depends on what you find works best for you, and also on the angle of the board, but in general the pen should be held steeply enough (about 60°) to allow you to write with the very tip of the nib. If the pen is held at too flat an angle, the pen will "stroke" the paper, rather than write on it, and the underside of the nib will be used, resulting in scratchy, uneven lines. Hold the pen with a relaxed grip; do not grasp it tightly.

You should look down directly on your writing, and move the work, rather than your hand, as you progress along the line, so that your writing hand remains in the correct position and your arm is free to move up and down. It may be easier to move your chair, rather than the paper, as you work – sitting at a long bench, or having a chair on wheels would solve the problem!

When starting work, first rule up the paper, then untape it, and fix the guard sheet in position. You will need a spare piece of paper for trying out the pen, and a rag, or tissues. A dip pen should be put together (*see pp38-9*) and then dipped or loaded from a brush (*see pp 40-1*). Try out the pen on your spare paper, and adjust the reservoir if necessary, or the board angle. The ink will start flowing most easily on a thin lead-in stroke. Use an even pressure on the whole of the nib; if you press more on one side, it will produce a ragged line. Occasionally wipe the pen to prevent the ink from drying on the nib.

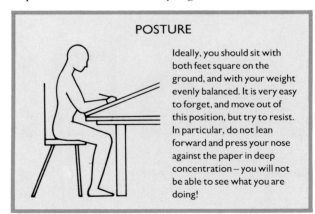

POSTURE

Ideally, you should sit with both feet square on the ground, and with your weight evenly balanced. It is very easy to forget, and move out of this position, but try to resist. In particular, do not lean forward and press your nose against the paper in deep concentration – you will not be able to see what you are doing!

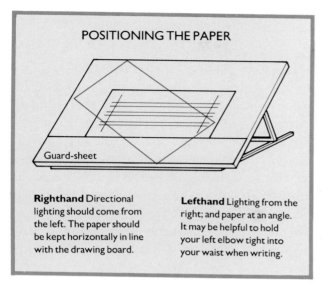

POSITIONING THE PAPER

Guard-sheet

Righthand Directional lighting should come from the left. The paper should be kept horizontally in line with the drawing board.

Lefthand Lighting from the right; and paper at an angle. It may be helpful to hold your left elbow tight into your waist when writing.

RULING UP

Ruling up paper can be time-consuming at first, but it is worth doing accurately, and once you have had some practice, it will get quicker. There are two short-cuts that you might find helpful at first: you can rule up a sheet of cartridge paper with a thin felt pen and use it as a guide beneath your writing paper if it is thin enough (tape the two together to keep the ruled paper in position); or you can buy ready-ruled papers.

Rule up for a baseline and the top of the x-height (or body height) of the letter. After some practice, allow yourself more freedom by ruling a baseline only.

There are several methods of ruling: with a parallel rule, a T-square, or using a ruler only; to mark off the height of the letters you can use dividers or simply mark off the divisions on a paper scale. Instructions are given here for ruling up a practice sheet for foundational hand. You will need: paper, masking tape, sharp pencil, T-square or ruler (optional: dividers, set square). The board should be flat.

First establish the x-height of the letter. Fill the pen with ink (if following the exemplar on p50, use a No. 1½ Mitchell nib, or equivalent), and on a scrap of paper mark off 4 full nib-widths. Set your dividers to this measurement, or mark off the measurement on the straight edge of a long piece of paper. (This will be used as a rule.)

Now take one sheet of layout paper and align the long edge of the paper on the board with the straight edge of the T-square and secure it at the corners with masking tape. (If you have a board with a parallel motion rule, align the paper in the same way.)

Using the dividers, or the paper rule, mark off the line widths accurately along one short side of the paper, keeping the marks very close to the edge of the paper. If using a ruler for the lines, you will have to mark the line widths down both sides of the paper (remembering to start at the same point!).

Now rule across. Keep the pencil sharp, use a light pressure and always hold the pencil vertical, keeping it close in to the edge of the T-square, otherwise line widths will vary. For a line space of 3 x-heights (or in other words, an interline space of 2 x-heights) rule up as shown.

To prevent yourself from writing to the very edge of the page, rule a couple of vertical margins on either side of the paper (about 2.5cm/1in from the edge) using a set square or ruler. Leave a generous margin at both top and bottom. Untape the paper before writing.

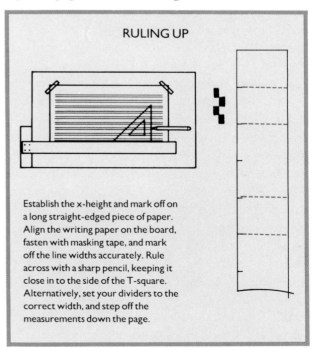

RULING UP

Establish the x-height and mark off on a long straight-edged piece of paper. Align the writing paper on the board, fasten with masking tape, and mark off the line widths accurately. Rule across with a sharp pencil, keeping it close in to the side of the T-square. Alternatively, set your dividers to the correct width, and step off the measurements down the page.

UNDERSTANDING THE SCRIPTS

IF YOU are impatient to start writing and you want quick results, then simply refer to the "key points" on the scripts pages, and copy the alphabets, following the order and direction of the strokes as shown. However, it is much more useful in the long term to understand the basic principles that can be applied to the letter forms in general, than to restrict yourself by copying individual letters one by one in alphabetical order. So take time to study the various points set out for each script, which stress the relationship and harmony of groups of letters and details. All the scripts (except copperplate on p62) are written with a broad-edged pen.

In time you will naturally develop your own writing style, as you will notice if you compare the variety of italic styles in the projects.

HISTORICAL EXAMPLE
Each example has been chosen to offer the most useful letter form for a particular style; while the alphabets have been adapted and modified (not directly "copied") from the examples, to provide a working model. This approach follows the method of study developed by Edward Johnston (1872-1944), the most notable of the early pioneers of the recent revival of calligraphy.

KEY POINTS
The most important points about each writing style are encapsulated here. Use them as starting points, relating to the particular alphabet given:
Basic form gives the key letter (generally "o") on which the rest of the alphabet is based. The essential form is most clearly seen when reduced to a "skeleton" (*see pp44-5 and pp52-3*), as it is affected by the angle and width of the edged pen.
Weight is determined by the relationship of the nib-width to the height of capital letters, or the "x-height" of minuscule (or lower-case) letters.
Pen angle is the angle of the pen nib in relation to the horizontal writing line, at which the pen is held for the majority of the strokes. Generally all horizontal, vertical and curved strokes keep to this angle. For diagonals the pen angle is generally altered in order to keep the width of letter strokes consistent. In general, the pen is steepened for left to right diagonals, and flattened for right to left diagonals.
Letter slope is the slope of the body of the letters in relation to the writing line.

ALPHABET
The order and direction of strokes, and change of pen angle are given. Refer to p44 for general rules.

LETTER GROUPS
Start by practising the letters in their main groups to give them a harmonious family resemblance, relating them in terms of shape, proportion and construction. This will also clarify your mental image of the letters so that you know what you are aiming at before you actually use your hand to write it.

RELATED PARTS
This looks more specifically at the details which are similar, or actually the same. Examine the way strokes overlap, how arches are joined to stems, the height of the ascenders and descenders, the type of serifs, the size of the

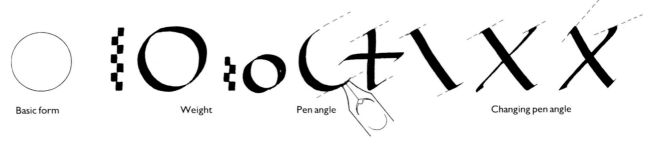

Basic form   Weight   Pen angle   Changing pen angle counters (interior space) in relation to the width of the stems and the whole letter.

ALTERNATIVE FORMS AND NUMERALS

Suggestions for alternative letter forms point the way towards learning to design your own letters. Numerals given for capitals (*see pp52-3*) and the foundational hand (*see pp50-1*) can be adapted for most scripts.

COMMON MISTAKES

When you are working on your own, it is very easy to repeat errors, and not be able to see what is going wrong; and it is surprising how the same ones keep on cropping up! A selection of the most commonly encountered errors are given here, to help you to identify your own problems. The mistakes relate only to their own alphabets – some of them may be perfectly acceptable for a different alphabet.

SPACING

Consistent spacing depends on well-written letters, and on developing a rhythm in your writing. The spacing suggested on p53 may be difficult for the modern eye (accustomed to the tight mechanical typographic spacing of newspaper headlines, for example) to accept, and so the hand fights against it too. But once you can space your letters in this way, you will be able to control any spacing system.

In general, to give an appearance of even letter spacing, place two straight-sided letters furthest apart, allow less distance between a vertical and a curve, and less still between two curves. Curved strokes introduce additional space between the letters and must therefore be slightly closed up to compensate. All other spacing combinations must be considered individually; each style has its own characteristics. As a guide, space between words should just accommodate an "o", although this depends on the hand; line space should be wider than letter space.

PLAN OF ACTION

1 Select a nib and rule up a large sheet of paper (see p47).

2 Write the letters in their main groups and study the related forms. Then go through the whole alphabet, referring to "common mistakes" if you have problems.

3 As soon as you feel confident with individual letter forms, write out a text that you like, so that you begin to think about how the letters actually relate.

4 Be aware of the spacing (inside and between the letters, and between the words). This can be seen more easily by standing well away from your work, or by looking at it reflected in a mirror. Try isolating small groups of letters by looking through a "window" made with your fingers, and compare the spacing.

5 It is a good idea to work at different speeds. Work slowly and carefully, assess your work, make any corrections, and then speed up, so that you start to develop rhythm and spontaneity.

6 Record your progress, by dating your work and making pencil notes of details such as nib sizes and x-heights.

7 As soon as possible, start working towards a finished piece of work on a good sheet of paper, and begin to consider layout. Start off with something simple, like a short quotation (see p70).

TEXT

A common text has been written, so that you can see the letters at work, and compare the pattern and character of each hand.

STUDYING OTHER STYLES

Armed with this information and method of study, you can learn any writing style that appeals to you. Find an example you like, and analyse it: identify the underlying form; the pen angle (look at the ends of straight strokes and the angle of the "thins" of curves); and the weight. To work out the weight, find the nib-width (usually at the widest part of a curved stroke), mark it off on a piece of paper, and use it as a scale to see how many times it will fit into the x-height of the letter. Then look at other points, such as the shape of the arches, the serifs, the letter slope, and the height of the ascenders and descenders.

FOUNDATIONAL

THE "Foundational" hand (also known as Round hand) was developed by Edward Johnston as a teaching hand, based on a 10th century manuscript in the British Library, London. It is a very useful starting point for Roman minuscule (or lower case) letters as it is based on the constant form of the circular "o" (which relates it to the Roman capitals).

The strong, simple, rounded forms should be studied from the modernized version given here; later you may want to make your own stylistic changes. At first, use a wide nib, or double pencils, and start with a line space of three times the x-height of the letter, so that the ascenders and descenders do not touch. For text written with an x-height of 4 nib-widths, use capitals from p52 at 6 nib-widths.

The Ramsay Psalter, written in southern England, circa AD 975. The actual x-height of letters is approximately 5mm (3/16in).

KEY POINTS

30°

(Use as a starting point for this exemplar.)
Basic form: circular "o".
Weight: 4 nib-widths (ascenders and descenders approx. 6½ nib-widths).
Pen angle: mainly 30°.
Letter slope: vertical.

Alphabet
a pen angle steepened.
b pen angle flattened slightly.
c pen angle flattened to 0°.
Nib size: No. 1½ Mitchell nib.

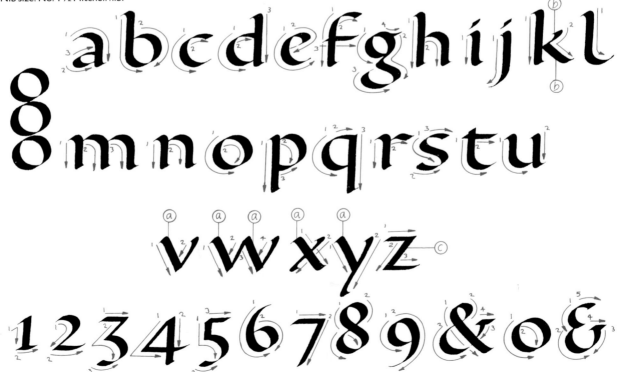

ocdqbp ahmnr

ltu

Letter groups Practise these two main letter groups first: **1** round letters (all related to the "o", but slightly narrower). **2** arched letters (related to the curves and proportion of the "o").

Related forms Arched letters are based on "o". The second stroke starts from inside the stem, giving a strong arch. The flattened curves strengthen the line of writing, making eye travel easier, and avoiding thickening of the joins in "d","p" and "q". The bowls of "e" and "a" should be of a similar size.

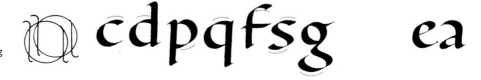 cdpqfsg ea

Alternative forms

aaggtxyy

Modifications Certain letter combinations produce spacing problems which can be solved by adjusting the letter forms. For instance, "r" can be shortened to tighten up the space; and double "f" can be written with one crossbar, making the second "f" slightly taller.

la ea ry ri fl ff tt

Common mistakes 1 Pen angle is too steep; **2** arch is too weak, it is just attached to the stem rather than starting from within it, and the curve is too square; **3** too narrow; **4** curve is not controlled and the stems should be straighter; **5** crossbar is too high, making the top of the letter look smaller than the bottom; **6** letter is too tall; **7** serif is too large and the exaggerated curve makes the letter lean backwards; **8** too narrow, giving pointed counters; **9** tail is not equally balanced beneath the bowl; the join between the bowl and the tail is too heavy, and the last stroke of the tail is too hooked; **10** too wide so letter appears to fall backwards.

n n n m m m
1 2 3 4

ff tt l l
5 6 7

ss gg ee
8 9 10

The flowers appear
on the earth; the time of
the singing of birds

51

ROMAN CAPITALS

MANY systems for analyzing classical Roman capitals have been devised; the geometric analysis of form and proportion shown here is based on studies made by Edward Johnston. Written with a broad-edged pen, these capitals are appropriate for use with Foundational hand, or Roman minuscule.

It is a very useful exercise to consider simplified "skeleton" forms of capital letters before using the edged pen, as it will give you a clearer understanding of their underlying structure. First, trace in pencil each of the skeleton letters from the various groups; write the letters more freely with pencil at the same size; then use an edged pen.

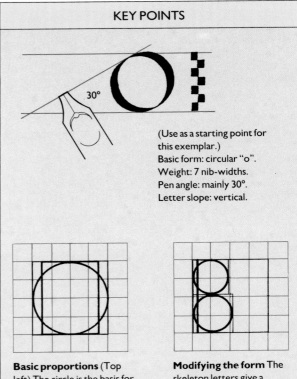

KEY POINTS

30°

(Use as a starting point for this exemplar.)
Basic form: circular "o".
Weight: 7 nib-widths.
Pen angle: mainly 30°.
Letter slope: vertical.

Basic proportions (Top left) The circle is the basis for the letter form. The rectangle (¾ the width of the square which contains the circle) is approximately the same area as the circle. (Top right) Approximately half the width of the square is occupied by a large group of narrow letters, whose curves are also based on circles.

Modifying the form The skeleton letters give a geometric framework from which to work. As soon as this is understood, the letters should be refined to give subtler forms with more visual harmony. The more weight added to the letter, the more adjustments must be made (such as widening "B", "P" and "R").

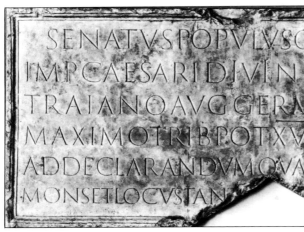

Alphabet
a pen angle steepened.
b pen angle flattened.
c pen angle flattened to 0°.
Nib size: No. 1½ Mitchell nib.

Trajan Column, Rome, AD 114. The actual height of letters is approx. 102mm (4in).

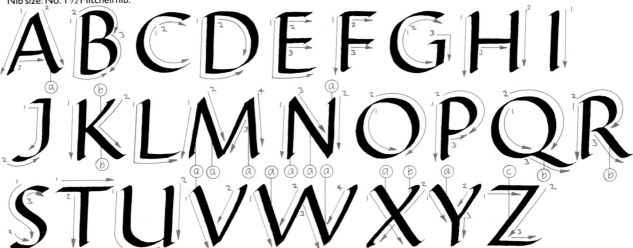

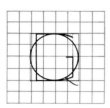

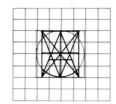

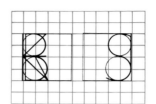

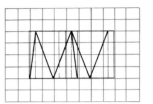

Letter groups in skeleton form
Round letters "O", "Q", "C", "G", "D" are based on the circle. Straight sides relate to the rectangle.

Rectangular-based letters "H", "N", "U", "T"; "A", "V", "X", "Y", "Z". Straight-sided and diagonal letters are contained within the rectangle.

Narrow letters "B", "P", "R", "E", "F", "L", "J", "S"; "K", "I" are based on a rectangular shape, approximately half the width of the square; curved shapes on circles, the bottom being larger to avoid "top-heaviness".

Wide letters: "M" is the width of the square (note the central "V" shape); "W" is very wide (based on two "V"s).

Related forms 1 These letters reflect the curve of "O". **2** The crossbars of "E", "F" and "H" rest on a central horizontal line; that of "A" hangs from it. **3** Diagonal joins should be as near to the end of the stems as possible to avoid thickening. Ensure that the joins of "M" are all the same height.

1 O C D B P R

2 A E F H   3 A N M V W

Common mistakes 1 Curves too "hooked", central curve should be straighter and thicker in the middle, letter leans backwards; **2** pronounced central curve gives a clumsy join; **3** diagonal stroke is too curved and joins badly, pen angle of legs is too flat; **4** serifs are part of the main stroke rather than being contained, the top arm is too thin; **5** the outer legs are splayed, thin strokes too thin, counters are uneven, letter not upright; **6** too straight at the top, too much thin pen line, shape and size of bowls uneven.

1 S S   2 P P   3 N N

4 K K   5 M M   6 B B

Numerals are written at the same height. The "0" is narrower than "O". All the curved numerals relate to this shape; counters should relate in size.

1 2 3 4 5 6 7 8 9 & 0

Spacing Aim for an even distribution of strokes, with a visually equal amount of space inside the letters and between them. Start with an average letter space of ⅝ of the width of the square. To achieve this, two vertical-sided letters should be spaced furthest apart (i.e. at ⅝); a curve and a vertical can be spaced a little closer; two curves have less distance between them; space other letters by eye. Word spacing should be just less than the width of an "O"; line space slightly more than this.

INNOCENT

THE FLOWERS
APPEAR ON THE EARTH;
THE TIME OF THE SINGING

53

UNCIALS

UNCIALS are an early pen-written letter form which preceded the development of small (or minuscule) letters, and so the hand is complete in itself, although the rudiments of ascenders and descenders can be seen in some of the letters. Uncials were used as a book hand (for writing out the text of manuscripts) between about the 5th and 8th centuries, and today it remains a suitable hand for writing long blocks of text due to the strong, even quality of the writing line that can be achieved. For capitals, write the same letter form at a larger scale, or use versals (*see pp56-7*).

Uncials are characterized by the wideness of the distinctive letter forms, and a very flat pen angle, which gives a strong horizontal movement to the letters. There is a wide variety of examples to choose from, many of which depend on a very complex handling of pen manipulation. The example given here is taken from a tiny, beautiful manuscript, whose letter forms are directly written in an elegant, restrained hand, thus providing a good starting point for understanding the basic characteristics of the script.

The St Cuthbert (Stonyhurst) Gospel of St John, written in the Wearmouth-Jarrow monasteries, England, circa AD 700. The actual x-height of letters is 2.5mm (3/16in).

KEY POINTS

(Use as a starting point for this exemplar.)
Basic form: "o" is wider than a circle.
Weight: 3½ nib-widths.
Pen angle: 15°.
Letter slope: vertical.

15°

Alphabet
a pen angle is steepened.
b pen angle is flattened.
Nib size: No. 1½ Mitchell nib.

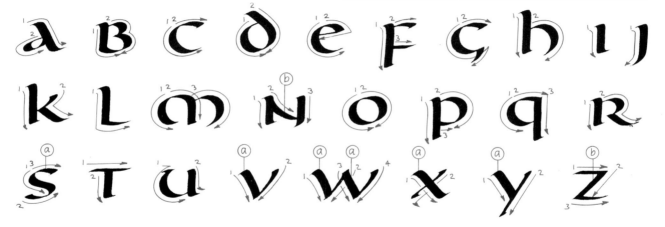

54

occeqdp
hmu
vwxy

Letter groups 1 Round letters: "o" is wider than a circle; the others relate to it. **2** Arched letters. **3** Diagonal letters: pen angle is steepened to give a greater contrast of stroke width.

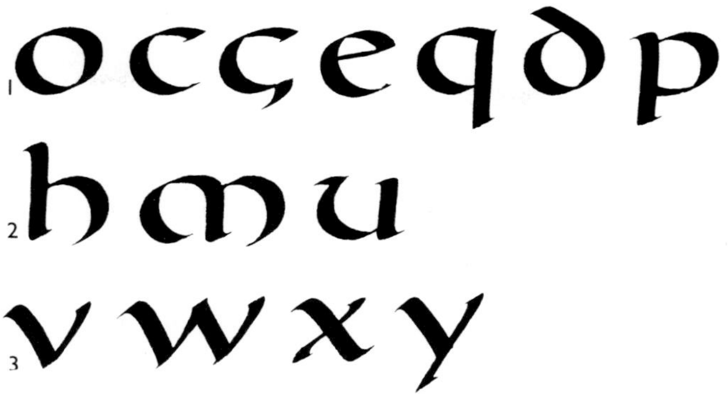

ouomqh
BR psf

Related forms 1 The curves of round and arched letters relate closely. **2** "B" and "R" echo these curves. **3** The lower curve of "P" and the top and bottom curves of "S" are flattened to avoid heaviness. The flattened top curves of "S" and "F" strengthen the writing line.

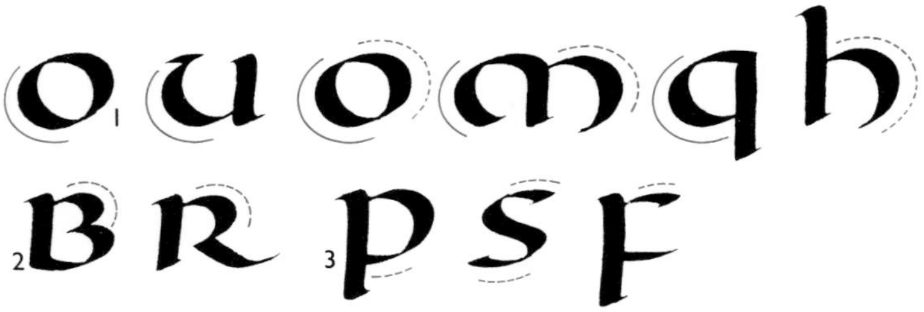

mm u u ff
nn k k x x

Common mistakes 1 The inside shapes are not balanced; **2** the weight sags to the bottom of the curve; **3** the crossbar is too low and the top curve too pronounced; **4** the diagonal bar is too low; **5** the diagonal should just touch the stem; **6** the pen angle has not been changed.

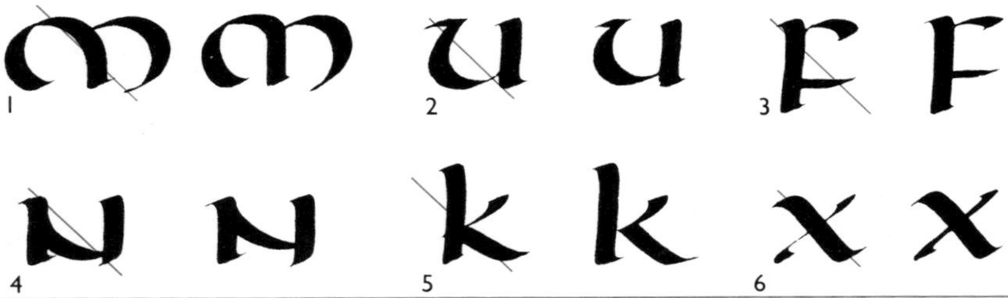

ᴅ ʜ

Alternative forms These alternative forms will give a stronger horizontal emphasis to the line of writing.

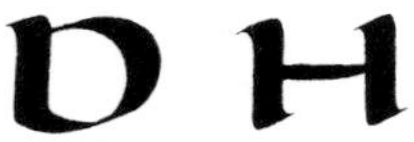

alphabet
alphabet
alphabet

Spacing 1 Close spacing gives an uneven pattern. **2** Wide spacing makes a word break up, thus weakening the line of writing and impairing legibility. **3** Correct spacing gives an even pattern of black and white, and enables the eye to move easily over the line of writing. The strength of the writing line depends on good letter forms and spacing, the line length, a generous line space, and an appropriate number of lines to a page.

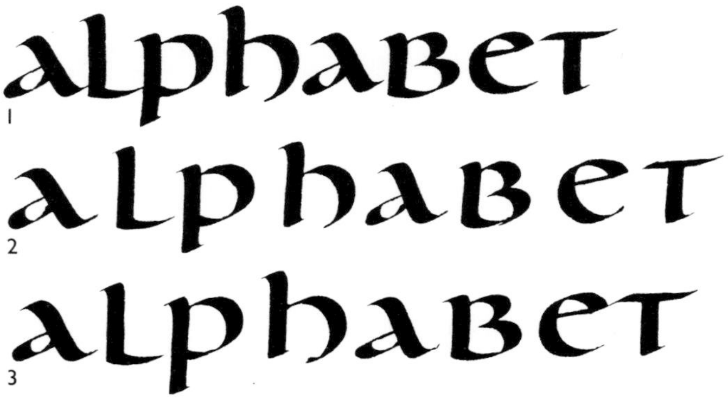

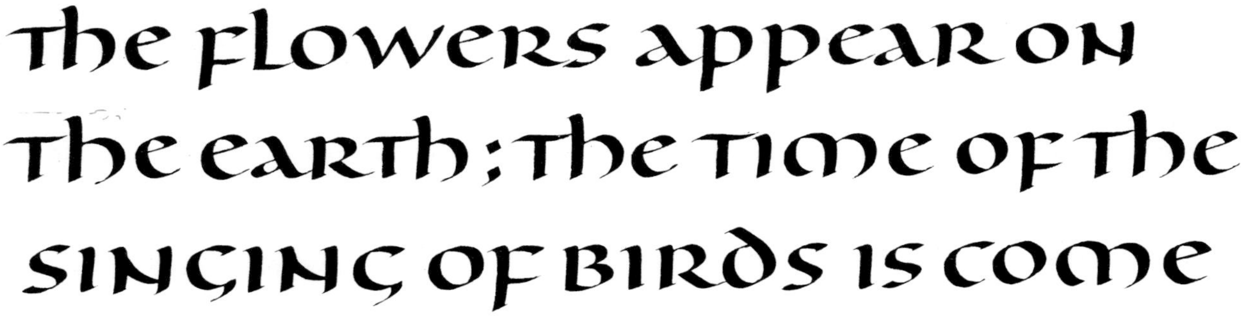

the flowers appear on the earth; the time of the singing of birds is come

55

VERSALS

THESE elegant capital letters are not directly written with a broad-edged pen, but are built up with a number of strokes, using a narrow edged pen or pointed brush. Their name reflects their original use as initial letters of verses or chapters of text, but they are frequently used for headings and are equally suitable for writing a block of text. These versatile letters can be used with most broad-edged scripts, and will give a distinctive contrast, particularly written in colour.

The alphabet below is written with open letters to demonstrate their construction more clearly. The letters shown here have a classical form, but many other forms and weights can be found, some of which can be used as the basis for illuminated letters (*see p100*).

(*see p100*)

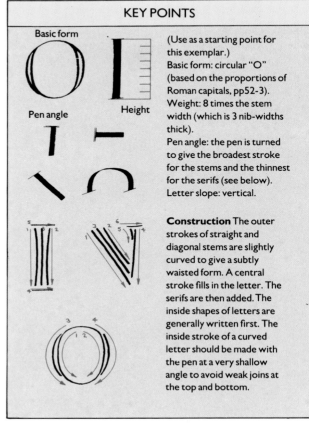

KEY POINTS

Basic form

Pen angle

Height

(Use as a starting point for this exemplar.)
Basic form: circular "O" (based on the proportions of Roman capitals, pp52-3).
Weight: 8 times the stem width (which is 3 nib-widths thick).
Pen angle: the pen is turned to give the broadest stroke for the stems and the thinnest for the serifs (see below).
Letter slope: vertical.

Construction The outer strokes of straight and diagonal stems are slightly curved to give a subtly waisted form. A central stroke fills in the letter. The serifs are then added. The inside shapes of letters are generally written first. The inside stroke of a curved letter should be made with the pen at a very shallow angle to avoid weak joins at the top and bottom.

Benedictional of St Aethelwold, written in England, circa AD 963-984 The actual height of letters is 1cm (⅜in).

Alphabet
Nib size: No. 4 Mitchell nib.

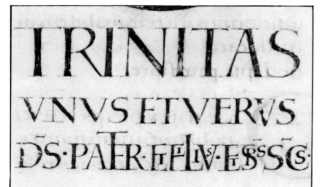

TRINITAS
VNVS ET VERVS
DS·PATER·ET·FILIVS·ET·SSC

A B C D E F G H I

J K L M N O P Q R

S T U V W X Y Z

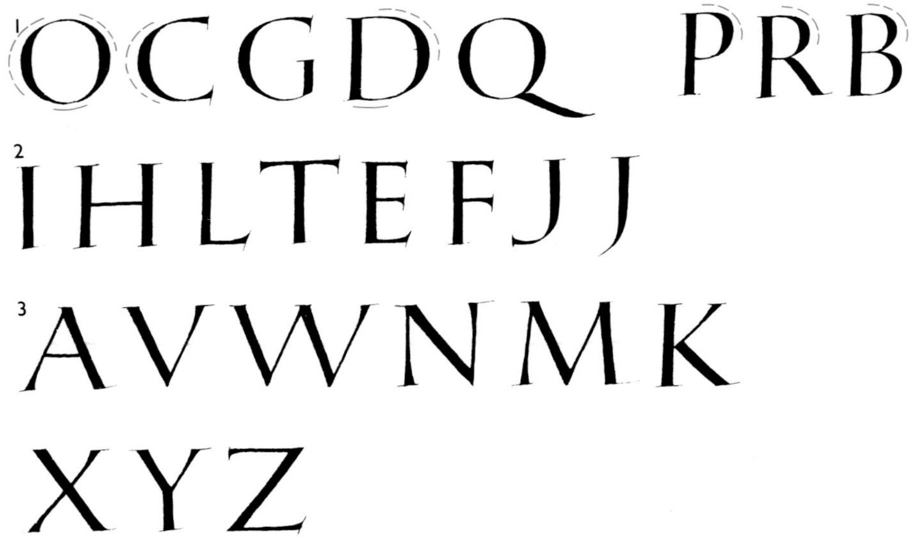

OCGDQ PRB

I H L T E F J J

A V W N M K

X Y Z

Letter groups Letters have been standardized to fall into the same groups as Roman capitals in terms of proportion, although in the manuscript the forms were adapted to make words fit the lines. They are arranged here to show related strokes. **1** Round letters all relate to "O"; "P", "R" and "B" also echo the shape. Curved strokes should be slightly wider at their thickest point than straight strokes so that they look visually equal. **2** Straight-stemmed. **3** Diagonal-stemmed.

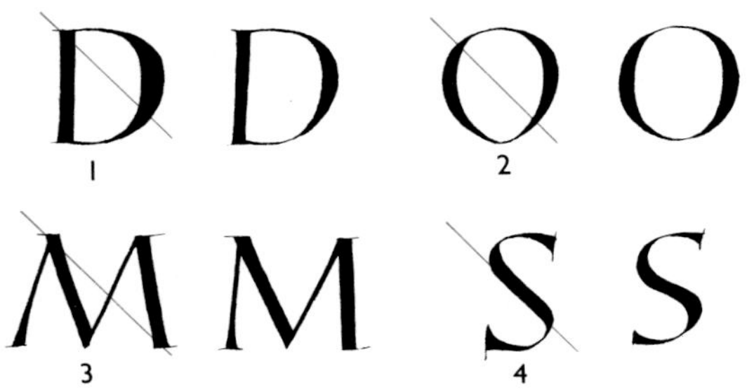

D D Q O

M M S S

Common mistakes 1 Straight and curved strokes are of an uneven thickness; **2** pointed "O" sets the wrong basic form for the alphabet; **3** the legs are too splayed and the top joins are at different levels; **4** inside shapes are pointed, top and bottom arms are too heavy.

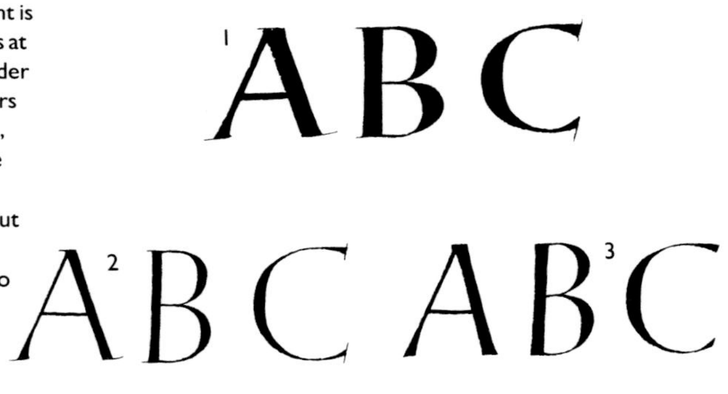

Initial letters Traditionally, versals introduce a block of text. Their position, however, varies:

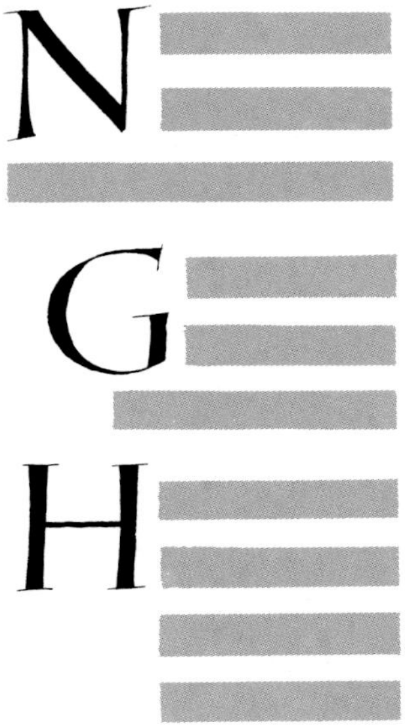

N

G

H

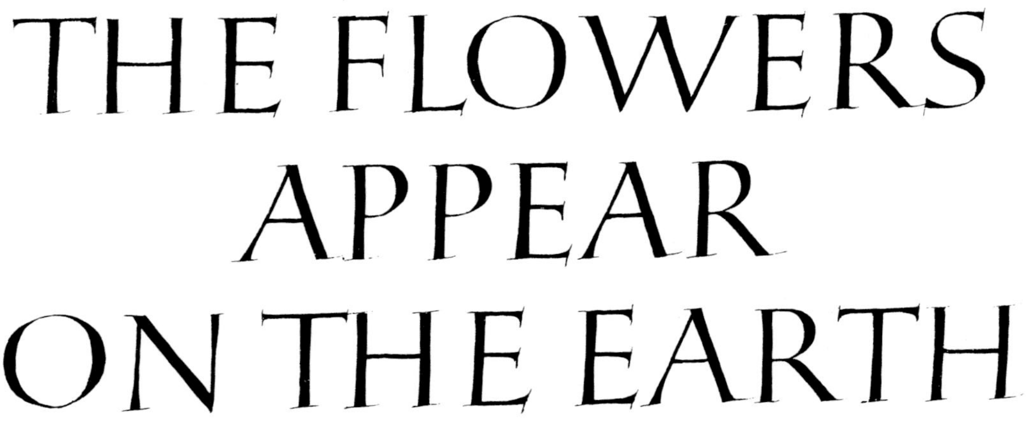

Variations 1 A heavier weight is achieved by writing the letters at the same height, but with a wider pen. **2** These lightweight letters are written at the same height, with a thinner nib (altering the height to stem width ratio). **3** Built-up letters written without serifs have a more modern appearance and lead the way to designing drawn letter forms.

A B C

A B C   A B C

THE FLOWERS
APPEAR
ON THE EARTH

57

GOTHIC

Tʜᴇ dense textural pattern of the compressed, angular letters of gothic manuscripts has given rise to the term "Black letter" to describe this style, which predominated from the 12th to the 15th century. Some of the subtleties of the historical example can only be achieved successfully with a quill, so the alphabet has been simplified for writing with a metal nib.

Gothic is not an ideal choice for a piece of work that has to put over information clearly, such as posters or menus, although it is popularly used for these – it is better suited to an occasion which calls for a decorative texture. It can be used with its own capitals or with versals.

Alphabets
Nib size: No. 1½ Mitchell nib.

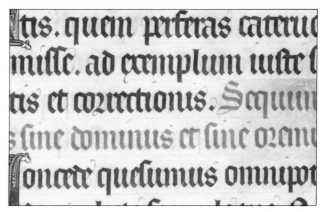

Metz Pontifical, written in northern France, circa 1300. The actual x-height of letters is 7mm (11/32in).

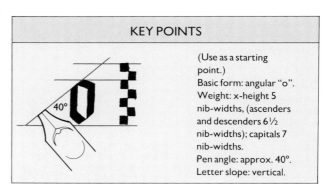

KEY POINTS

(Use as a starting point.)
Basic form: angular "o".
Weight: x-height 5 nib-widths, (ascenders and descenders 6½ nib-widths); capitals 7 nib-widths.
Pen angle: approx. 40°.
Letter slope: vertical.

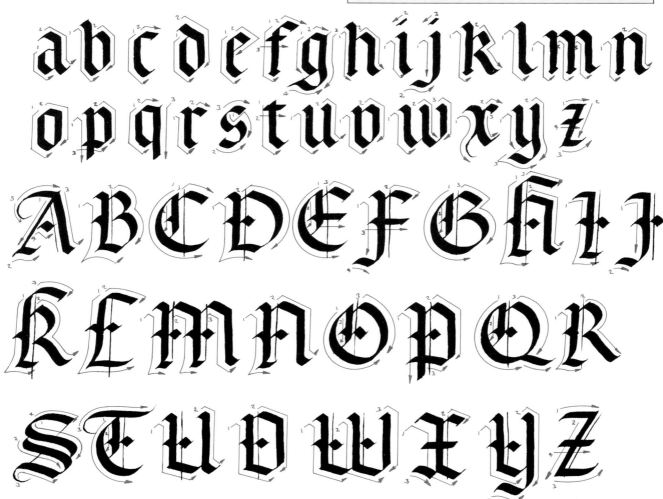

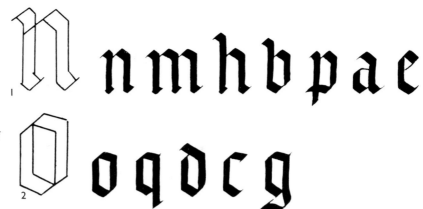

Letter groups Arched letters can be practised in two groups, which differ in the construction of the join: **1** the arch leaves the stem with a thin joining stroke at a steep angle; **2** a flattish top arch is taken from the corner of the preceding stroke.

Related forms 1 Straight strokes should be made in one movement with the pen at a constant angle, pausing where the stroke changes direction. (The historical example has a slight change of angle). The turns should start at about one nib-width from the top or bottom of the x-height. **2** Feet: the first is shorter and the second more pronounced. **3,4** The vertical stress and the regularity of the counter spaces give gothic its characteristic appearance.

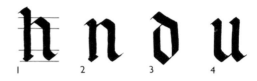

Common mistakes 1 Counter spaces too wide or uneven —they should be just slightly wider than the stems; **2,3** overall width of the letter is too wide; **4** the first stroke turns too low down; **5** the ascender is too long, interrupting the strong texture of the script —an additional 1 or 1½ nib-widths above the x-height is adequate.

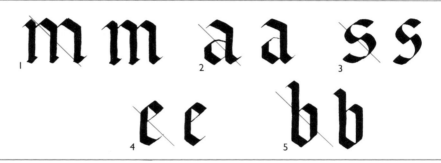

Shared stems The compactness of this hand can be further emphasized by combining two letters, so that they share stems. Additionally, in gothic manuscripts, words are often abbreviated, or broken arbitrarily in an attempt to keep a strong right hand margin, and to give the page an even textural pattern.

Spacing The space inside the letters should be visually equal to the space between the letters. The short ascenders and descenders allow a short line space which will emphasize the textural quality of the hand. The text below changes to Latin in the second line to illustrate the point that texture is a more dominant feature of the hand than legibility.

The flowers appear on the earth tempus putationis advenit; vox turturis audita est in terra nostra

ITALIC

THE italic hand was developed in Italy during the Renaissance as a cursive style to meet the demand for a quickly written, elegant letter, and also as a reaction against the heaviness of gothic letter forms. In comparison to earlier scripts, italic is characterized by a steepened pen angle, a greater letter slope, and springing arches which reduce the number of strokes per letter, giving the hand a fluidity and rhythm which makes it highly legible. The historical example shows a good basic form to follow. The capitals are a compressed, slightly sloping and informal adaption of Roman capitals.

Alphabets
Nib size: No. 1½ Mitchell nib.
a pen angle steepened.
b pen angle flattened.

Et hor col freno tuo santo correggi
Il lungo error de le mie uoglie ar⌐
on lasciar la mia guardia, et nor
La tua pieta ; perchio tolto a le leg
M'habbia d'amor, et disturbato i

Bembo's sonnets, written in Italy, circa 1543. The actual x-height of letters is 2mm (1/16in).

KEY POINTS	
45°	(Use as a starting point.) Basic form: "a". Weight: x-height 5 nib-widths, (ascenders and descenders 9 nib-widths); capitals 7 nib-widths high. Pen angle: 45°. Letter slope: about 5°.

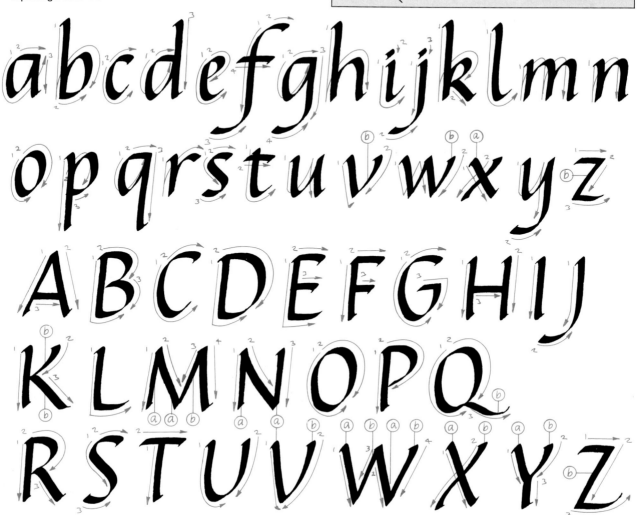

Letter groups The shape of the key letter "a" should be practised first. It is made in three strokes: the first, which is a straightened curve, should spring up from the bottom to the top of the x-height, thus breaking the rule of not "pushing" the pen; the two strokes are parallel.
1 Superimpose "d", "g", and "q" on "a"; "b" and "p" echo this shape, but start with a clockwise stroke. **2** "n", "h", "m", and "r" have arches written in a clockwise direction; "u" and "y" begin in an anticlockwise direction. **3** These are based on a more oval shape, but occupy the same space.

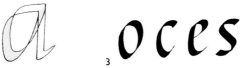

Related forms 1 Arched letters branch just above the mid point. Note the triangular space at the top of the letter. **2** The triangular notch at the bottom of the letter is slightly larger. The up-swept strokes are pushed, using a springing touch. **3** Curved letters should have a straightness to them. Relate the curves of all the thin strokes. **4** The crossbars should hang from the top of the x-height. Note the similarity of these curves.

Alternative letter forms

Common mistakes 1 Pen angle is too steep, taking the weight to the top and bottom of the letter; **2** the letters do not relate – "a" is too round, the second part of "m" is too narrow; **3** the letter, and the crossbar are both too high; **4** the letter is too round, and the bottom stroke of the bowl starts too high up.

Spacing Start with generous spacing – the cursive quality of this hand will give a rhythmical quality to a piece of writing, even if the spacing is wide. Aim for a certain straightness in the curved letters and an even distribution of space inside and outside the letters. The ascenders and descenders, and the character of the script demand wide line spacing and generous margins.

COPPERPLATE

THE CONTRAST between the thick and thin strokes of this strongly slanted style of writing is achieved by applying pressure with a pointed flexible pen. Developed from the italic hand, many varieties of the style were in use from the 16th to the 18th century. Its general name is taken from the method used to reproduce the letters, which involved engraving on copper plates. The version shown is also referred to as English Round Hand. The pen must be held differently from the way it is held for broad-edge letter styles, which is to the advantage of left-handers. Achieving the characteristic fluidity of the style requires a light touch.

Engraved by George Bickham, London 1743. From *The Universal Penman* (reproduced same size).

PEN HOLD

The pen must be held so that it points in the direction of the stroke being made. Left-handers can hold the pen naturally in the correct way, but right-handers should turn the paper to a steep angle on the board to avoid twisting the hand at an uncomfortable angle (an elbow-joint pen will avoid this problem).

Left-handed   Right-handed

Alphabet
Nib: Gillott 404. A dot marks the beginning of the stroke. Change pen angle for "Z".

● pressure

○ no pressure

Key points/strokes

(Use as a starting point.)

Basic form: oval "o".

Weight: x-height of lower-case letters approx. 7 times the widest pen stroke; (ascenders and descenders twice the x-height); capitals slightly taller than the ascenders.

Angle of pen: points in direction of letter slope.

Letter slope: approx. 55°.

Thick strokes are made with pressure on strokes pulled towards you; thin strokes are light upstrokes. For lower-case letters, it is useful to start by practising letter strokes which are common to a group of letters.

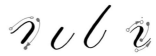

1 Oval, with pressure on left side (as in "a", "c", "d", "e", "g", "o" and "q").

2 Curved arches in a clockwise direction; an anticlockwise direction; a double curve (as in "b", "j", "i", "k", "l", "m", "n", "p", "t", "u", "v", "w" and "y").

3 Long strokes (for ascenders and descenders) ending with a curve; beginning with a curve; a long double curve.

4 Straight strokes, written with firm, even pressure (as in "k" and "q").

5 Light upstrokes and joining strokes (as in "f", "i", "j", "p", "r", "t", "v", "w" and "y").

6 Dots are made in a tiny spiral movement in either direction.

Numerals

$ £ ? !

Height

The same nib can be used to write letters at a wide range of size and weight. All these letters were written with a Gillott No. 404 nib, using varying pressure on the downstrokes.

Common mistakes

1 Letters too narrow, and too close; **2** letters too heavy, the change from thick to thin too abrupt. **unbalanced**: "un" – uneven; "b" – ascender too tall and broad; "a" – too narrow and heavy; "l" – ascender too tall and broad; "a" – curved stroke too flattened; "d" – too narrow, top curve too flat, ascender too tall and broad.

Touching up The ends of broad strokes can be sharpened up with the pen.

Spacing

The extreme contrast of thick and thin strokes, and the fact that the hairline ligatures that connect the letters are an integral part of the letter forms themselves, demand a fresh look at spacing. **1** Aim for an even pattern of thick and thin, and space outside and within the letter. **2** The ligatures should flow comfortably. **3** Accommodate the different visual spaces created by fine and broad lines. Thus, two adjacent broad strokes need more space between them than a fine and a broad stroke.

The flowers appear on the earth; the time of the singing of birds is come, and the voice of the turtle is heard in our land. The Song of Solomon·

DESIGN

GUIDELINES and general advice about design can be helpful, but it is more important for you to understand and develop the ideas in a practical way. Thus, you will learn much more if you first learn to look about you and teach yourself to really "see".

The "gallery" section has already given you some idea of how varied design can be, while the projects give practical instructions for following a range of designs. On this page, some of the points covered in the projects are drawn together, to suggest a more general method of approach.

To broaden your feeling for design in general, and your visual awareness, start training yourself to become really observant of everything around you: look at posters, shop signs, paintings, the silhouette of trees and buildings against the skyline, or flower structures. Keep a sketchbook, and in a scrapbook collect samples of advertisements, and examples of calligraphy and type. Consciously try to become more discerning about your visual appreciation.

CALLIGRAPHIC DESIGN

Calligraphic design has a more specific starting point – it concerns the visual expression of words. A sensitive response to words, language and communication, and a passion for reading will give the calligrapher a head start.

The starting point, of course, is the words themselves, what you want (or have) to say, or show with them, and why you are doing it at all! Do not underestimate the importance of these considerations. For instance, the type of work you would produce to a tight guideline for a client, using a given wording, and to fit a given area will be approached in a very different manner from a piece of calligraphy that is done purely for personal satisfaction, and which does not even have to be clearly legible.

Some people are fortunate enough to have a clear visual picture of the arrangement of a piece of work before they even begin (and often the first idea remains the best solution). If you are unsure of your intentions before you start, it is helpful to think in terms of building on what you do know. It is useful to begin with the choice of letter forms.

LETTER FORMS AND LINE ARRANGEMENT

Most people have some kind of intuitive awareness of the identity and associations of various lettering styles; for instance, the difference in mood and period between gothic and copperplate writing (of course, this is also influenced by nationality). However, although it is useful to have a full "vocabulary" of scripts, an ability to handle three basic scripts (capitals, foundational, and italics, for instance) will probably carry you through most situations at the outset.

Each letter form has its own pattern and rhythm (compare the common text on pp 50-63). By introducing a simple variety in the weighting, spacing, and arrangement of the letters, you can begin to experiment with layout.

Letter weight can be varied by altering the x-height (*see p70*), or by keeping a constant x-height and changing the width of the nib (*see p74*), or by using colour.

Letter spacing, word spacing and line spacing can also be changed to vary the textural quality of a piece of work (*see p70*). Remember, that as soon as two letters are put down next to each other, the spacing system is set for that particular area of text.

Line length is determined by the nature of the text and the purpose of the piece. If the lines are broken, this is best done where there is literally a "pause for breath" (such as at the end of a phrase), so that the sense and rhythm of the words are not altered. However, lines can also be arranged in such a way as to deliberately alter the sense, or reading speed. At the extreme, sense, and sometimes legibility, can be purely secondary to the visual pattern that lines make.

The arrangement of lines is most conveniently referred to in typographic terms (*see box*).

FORMAT AND EMPHASIS

The format of a piece of work is generally determined at an early stage, often by a feeling for the text. The two most common formats are landscape (horizontal) and portrait (vertical), although obviously any shape can be used. For work that is done to commission, the format is sometimes predetermined, so the design must be made to work within it.

Consider the overall shape of the text and balance it with the empty space and the margins, which all play a very positive part in the design. In addition, sort out the order of importance of all the various parts of your design – the heading, author, texts, and so on – and decide on the emphasis you want to give each one, to determine its dominance in the design.

The degree to which you play around with the arrangement, contrast and emphasis is generally determined by your attitude to the words. You may want to write the words as simply as possible, to let them speak for themselves; or perhaps you will want to impose on them a more personal interpretation. This is for you to decide. However, a piece that serves a functional purpose must state its message clearly.

Materials and colour have a powerful and evocative impact. A design that has been worked out with pen and ink on layout paper will be totally transformed by the use of colour, or a good quality paper, so consider this early on.

The finishing touch – mounting and framing – will also affect the design, and, in general will enhance it considerably.

WORKING ORDER

You will soon settle into your own way of working, but the following is a suggested approach for a simple layout:

Start by reading the text several times and then write it out very simply, in a style and size that you are happy using. Consider all the points listed below, cut up the lines of text, and arrange them on a sheet of paper, deciding on a suitable format for the words. Then start to develop areas of emphasis and contrast, but be selective – remember that there is beauty in simplicity..

DESIGN CHECK LIST

1 What do the words say to you?

2 What is your purpose in doing it?

3 Who are you doing it for?

4 What form will it take?

5 Where will it be seen?

6 Does a format suggest itself? If this is already decided, then how will you make the most of it?

7 What is a suitable script?

8 How many different elements (or categories of information) are involved; which is the most, and least, important?

9 What materials should you use?

10 Will you use colour?

11 Should illustration or other decoration be incorporated?

PASTE-UP AND PREPARING FOR PRINT

You will gradually develop a way of working that suits you. You might begin a piece with a thumbnail sketch pencilled on the back of an envelope, and then develop it in stages to its conclusion, or you might begin with a full-size rough, written with edged pens, that is very close to the finished version.

It is important to be flexible about the evolution of a design; using "paste-up" as a method of working will encourage this. Cut up your text and arrange it, like pieces of a jigsaw, rewriting, and repositioning the pieces until the best solution is found. Then glue them in position.

There are several glues you can use, including glue sticks, rubber cement and spray glue. Rubber cement is the most popular among calligraphers. Use a flat plastic spreader to give a very thin film of glue on both surfaces of the paper and allow it to dry for a couple of minutes before contact. Spray glue is extremely convenient and efficient, but the airborne glue particles are a health hazard. Both rubber cement and spray glue allow for repositioning of the paper for some time afterwards. Glue sticks are handy, but do not easily allow for repositioning.

The shadows cast by strips of paper can give a slightly inaccurate impression of line space. To some extent this can be overcome by looking at the design through a sheet of layout, or tracing paper, pressed down over the paste-up.

The final paste-up can be used as a ruling guide for the finished piece. Transfer the baseline measurements on to a "paper scale" (a piece of paper with a straight edge), and use this as a ruler to mark out the lines on a new sheet of paper (*see p79*), remembering to consider the margins. Now write out the text as one piece, using the paste-up as a guide for the position of the beginning and end of the lines. Often, any final design problems can be ironed out now. Adjustments can be made and the piece re-ruled for a final version.

If you have to fit a certain number of lines within a specified area at regular intervals, there is a simple method of dividing up the paper, without having to work it out mathematically (*see box*).

PREPARING FOR PRINTING

Calligraphy can be printed from a paste-up of the work, as can be seen in several of the projects in the book. This obviously makes work easier, as the whole piece does not have to be written perfectly at one time, and it allows for corrections and easy line positioning. It also means that work can be reduced to any size required.

For small quantities, such as greetings cards, photocopying might prove to be a cheaper alternative. This can be done on paper or card of a variety of colours.

The most common method of printing today is done photographically by offset-lithography. Line printing will reproduce solid lines only; a half-tone print will pick up any tonal change. The effect of a tonal print can be achieved by printing a tint of a colour. This is done by the printer who lays a screen over the area, breaking it up with a pattern of white dots (to whatever percentage of the solid colour is required).

Work is generally sent to the printer as black and white "artwork", which is then printed with ink of any colour requested. Calligraphy using

CENTRING

For a centred arrangement, fold the lines of writing in half and position on the line.

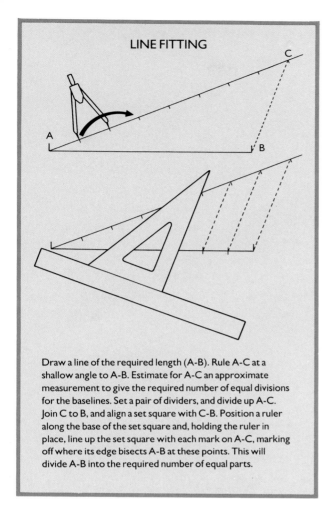

LINE FITTING

Draw a line of the required length (A-B). Rule A-C at a shallow angle to A-B. Estimate for A-C an approximate measurement to give the required number of equal divisions for the baselines. Set a pair of dividers, and divide up A-C. Join C to B, and align a set square with C-B. Position a ruler along the base of the set square and, holding the ruler in place, line up the set square with each mark on A-C, marking off where its edge bisects A-B at these points. This will divide A-B into the required number of equal parts.

A paste-up for printing should be done on board, or on strong cartridge paper. Use a blue non-reproducing crayon or a light pencil line for ruling. When you have settled on your final design, clean off the glue with an eraser of dried rubber cement, and give it a final clean up with lighter fuel. The cut lines will not show if they have been tidied up. It is best to check by getting a PMT done, as you can then "white out" any marks with white gouache, correction fluid, or a PMT eraser pen. Otherwise, ask the printer to do this for you.

Define the edge of the paper clearly by drawing trim marks at the corners, and if the paper is to be folded, draw dotted lines to mark the fold. The trim marks must be broken at their axis to avoid being printed. An overlay of layout paper, tracing paper or film acetate will protect your work. You can also write instructions on it.

Instructions to the printer should include the following: your name and address; the date required; the quantity required; the colour of ink; the colour, weight and type of paper; final size (and, if appropriate, instructions for reduction); a warning if the ink is non-waterproof.

colour can be reproduced in full colour, but this is much more expensive.

It is useful to find out as much as you can about printing techniques if you intend to do much work for reproduction. In general, however, it is best to find a reliable printer who will be able to advise you. It is worth bearing in mind that the better you prepare your work for the printer, the better are your chances of getting good results.

The printer can reduce or enlarge work by a process known as a PMT (photo-mechanical transfer); it can also be "reversed", so that what is written in black on white will appear as white writing on black.

Working on a larger scale, and getting your work reduced to the size required can help to sharpen up the letter forms, but be careful – too much reduction tends to alter the weight and spacing of letters. Before having work printed at a reduced size, make a reduced photocopy.

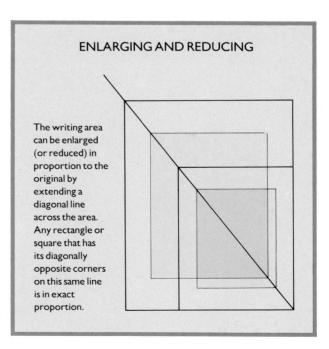

ENLARGING AND REDUCING

The writing area can be enlarged (or reduced) in proportion to the original by extending a diagonal line across the area. Any rectangle or square that has its diagonally opposite corners on this same line is in exact proportion.

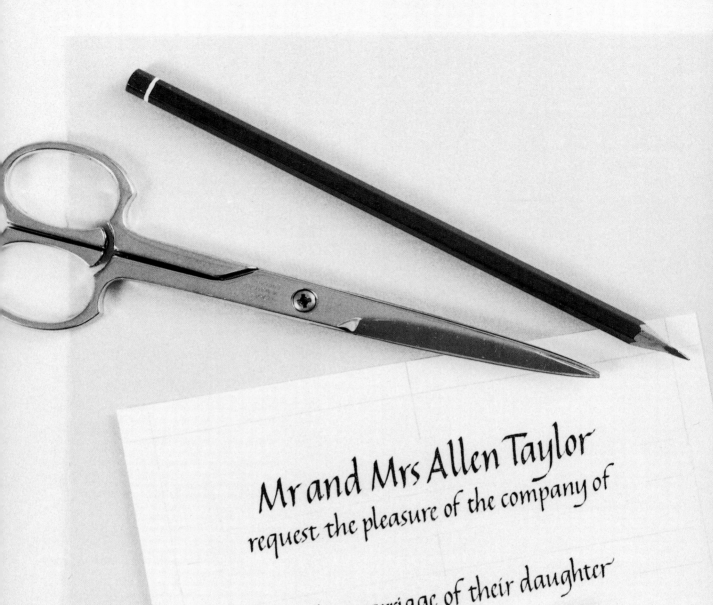

Mr and Mrs Allen Taylor
request the pleasure of the company of

at the marriage of their daughter

Charlotte

to

Mr David Beckett

on Saturday 4th October at 3 p.m.

at All Saints Church, Fulham

Practical Calligraphy

The projects can be followed as a course, or selected at random. The first two link closely with the previous section. A series of projects prepared for printing is followed by some of greater complexity in terms of technique or design. Drawn letters are introduced; a series of simple hand-printing methods offer some interesting alternatives; and a final experimental section encourages you to explore your own style. At the top of the box on the first page of each project a section of the finished piece is shown at actual size to give a sense of scale.

A Quotation

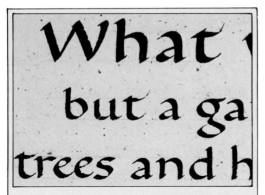

Foundational hand and capitals, written with Mitchell round hand nibs: No. 1½ nib; No. 2½ nib.

What was an orchar full of ple

No. 2½ nib. X-height of letters 3½ nib-widths.

What wa an orchar of pleasu

No. 2½ nib. X-height of letters 4 nib-widths.

What wa garden, a and herb

No. 2½ nib. X-height of letters 4½ nib-widths.
All lettering in this box is actual size.

START off with something simple – a favourite quotation, a short extract from a poem or a piece of prose – to mark your first achievements in calligraphy, which can be kept simply as a reminder, framed and proudly displayed, or given as a gift. Use the script that you feel most confident with (foundational hand is an excellent starting point), and decide on one constant design factor. Here it is the symmetrical centred arrangement, while other aspects, such as letter weight/height, line length and line space are varied.

Centring by eye is tricky, and takes practice, but it can be made easier by using paste-up. You will need: basic equipment (*see pp36-7*), and a piece of good paper (in this case, Indian handmade).

What was paradise, but a garden an orchard of trees and herbs, full of pleasure, and nothing there but delights.

Letters written with an x-height of 3½ nib-widths.

What was paradise, but a garden, an orchard of trees and herbs, full of pleasure and nothing there but delights

Letters written with an x-height of 4 nib-widths.

What was paradise, but a garden, an orchard of trees and herbs, full of pleasure and nothing there but delights

Letters written with an x-height of 4½ nib-widths.

I An x-height (or body height) of 4 nib-widths is a good starting point for foundational hand. The line space is 2½ times the x-height of the letter (from baseline to baseline), closer than that shown on page 51. Rule up on layout paper for writing with the same nib at the three different weights shown above. Paste-ups can be made from this, or from photocopies of your writing.

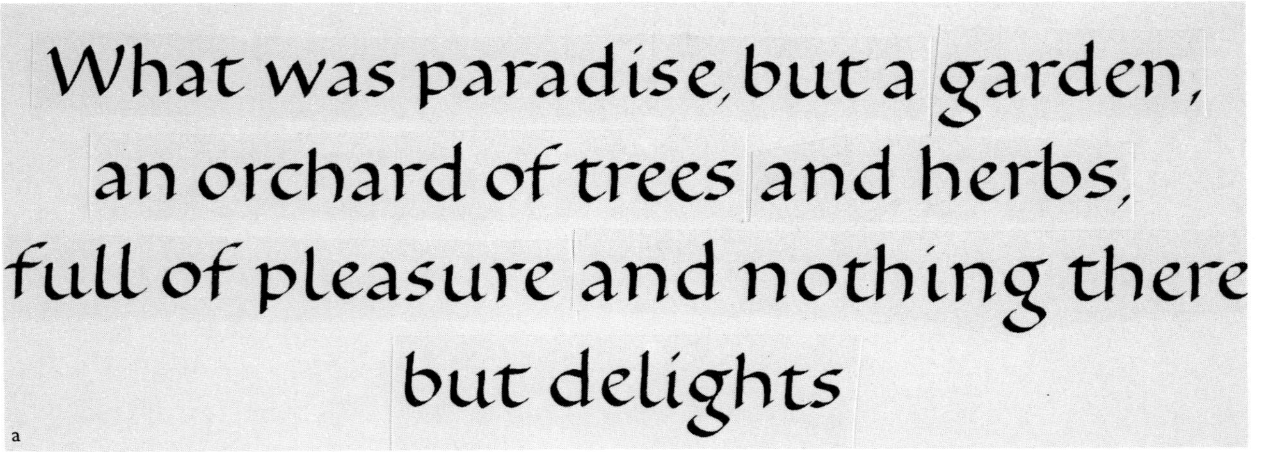

What was paradise, but a garden,
an orchard of trees and herbs,
full of pleasure and nothing there
but delights

a

2 Foundational hand lends itself to long, well-spaced lines.
Think of the phrasing of the words as you cut up the lines.
a is at 4½ nib-widths, with a line space of 3 times the
x-height. Long lines generally require generous line spacing.

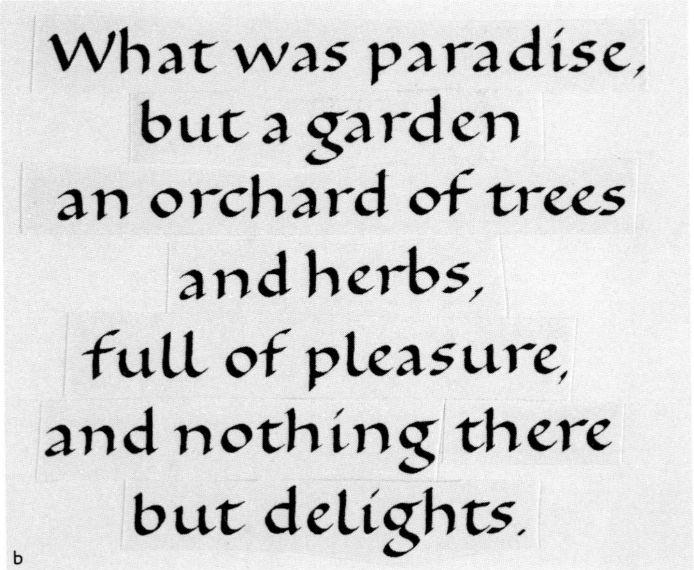

What was paradise,
but a garden
an orchard of trees
and herbs,
full of pleasure,
and nothing there
but delights.

b

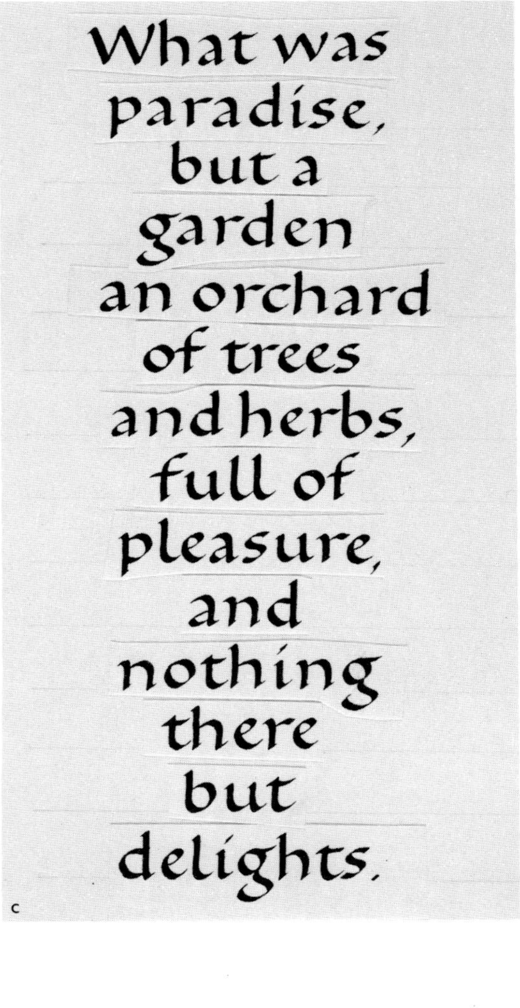

3 A heavier letter weight **b** (3½ nib-widths) forms a denser
pattern, which can suit an arrangement over shorter lines,
and, with the reduction in the line space (2½ x-heights), a
good balanced arrangement is achieved. In **c** the line space is
slightly closer, giving a darker pattern.

Letter weight, line length and line space all have an effect
on the reading pace: longer lines allow for more continuous
reading, whereas the text arrangement on the right, places
more emphasis on pattern than on legibility.

What was
paradise,
but a
garden
an orchard
of trees
and herbs,
full of
pleasure,
and
nothing
there
but
delights.

c

71

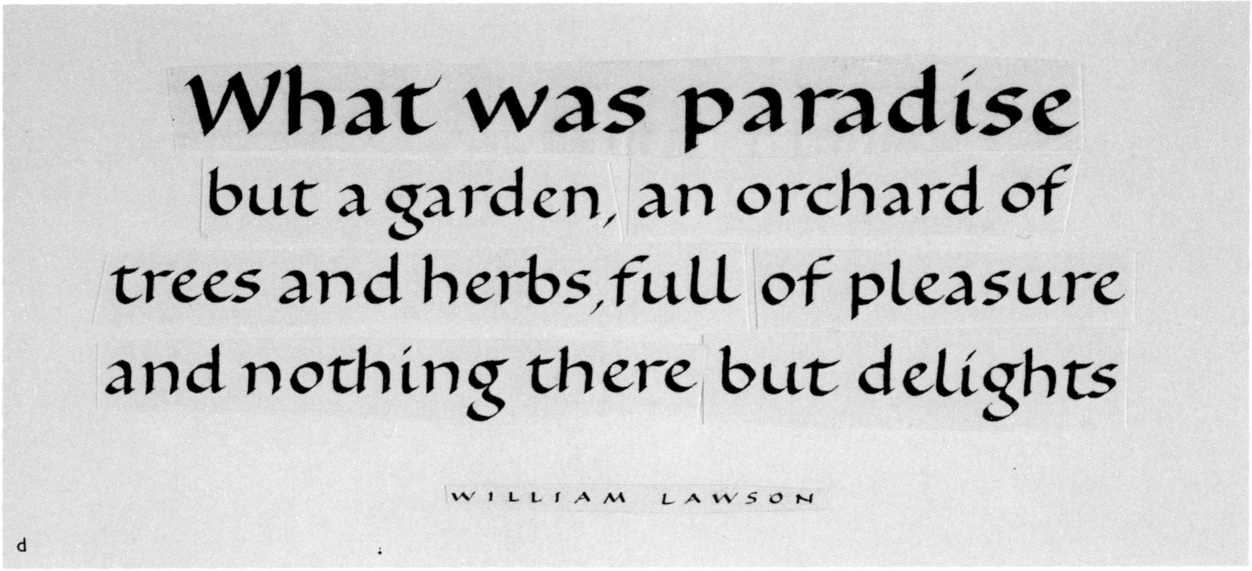

What was paradise
but a garden, an orchard of
trees and herbs, full of pleasure
and nothing there but delights

WILLIAM LAWSON

d

4 Emphasis is changed **d** by writing the opening words with a wider nib
(1 $\frac{1}{2}$ at 4 nib-widths high), keeping the same line space as before. The name
of the author is used to balance the design, and give a pleasing contrast.

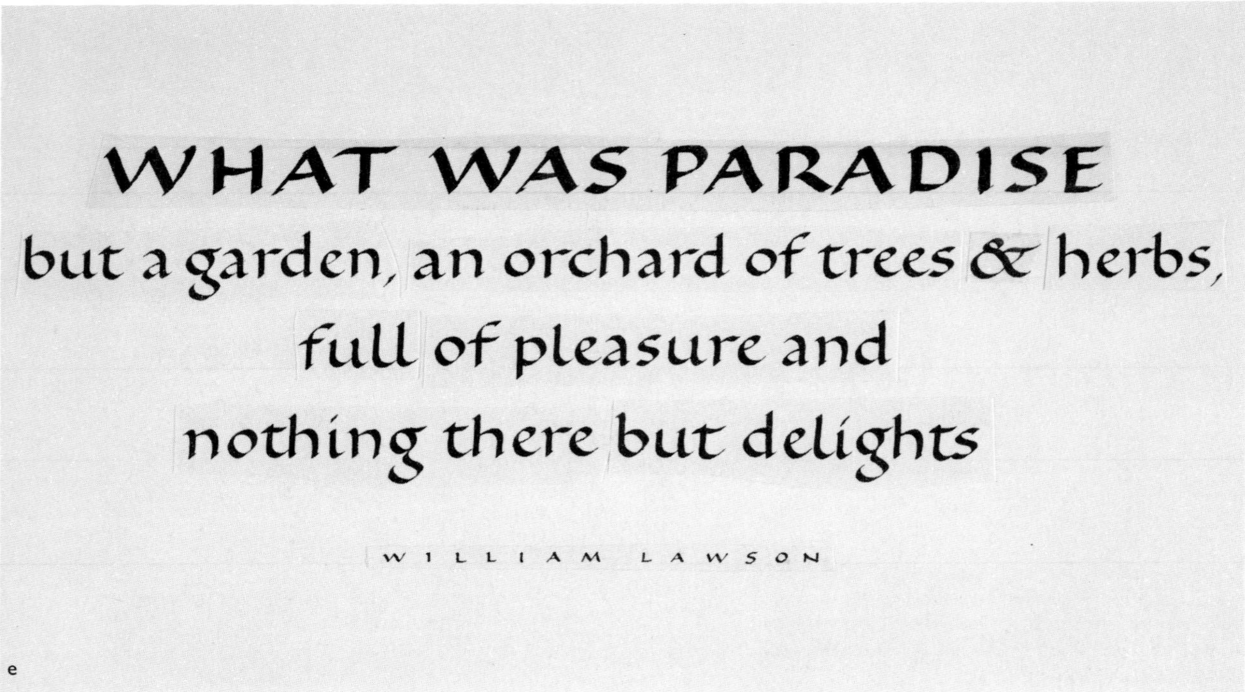

WHAT WAS PARADISE
but a garden, an orchard of trees & herbs,
full of pleasure and
nothing there but delights

WILLIAM LAWSON

e

5 Using the same nib, the top line is written in capitals. The greater variety
in line length gives an interesting pattern, however, the third line does not
read well. Always allow plenty of space around the text, and determine the
margins by placing two large L-shaped pieces of paper over the work so
that you can visualize the overall effect.

> ## What was paradise
> but a garden an orchard of trees
> and herbs, full of pleasure,
> and nothing there
> but delights.

6 This centred arrangement has a rather top-heavy, tapered appearance which is not particularly well balanced. It is worth, however, investigating several possibilities before deciding on the final design.

> ## What was paradise
> but a garden, an orchard of
> trees and herbs, full of pleasure
> and nothing there but delights.
>
> WILLIAM LAWSON

7 Mark off the measurements from the selected rough (d) on to a paper scale (see p79), and then transfer them on to good paper. Rule up, allowing generous margins. Mark in pencil where the lines should begin and end. Use your rough as a guide for spacing, folding it up so that as you write, each line is directly visible. Try to relax so that your writing does not lose its fluidity. The piece can now be framed.

Actual size: 14 × 25cm (5½ × 9¾in).
Calligraphy by Patricia Gidney.

73

CHRISTMAS CARD

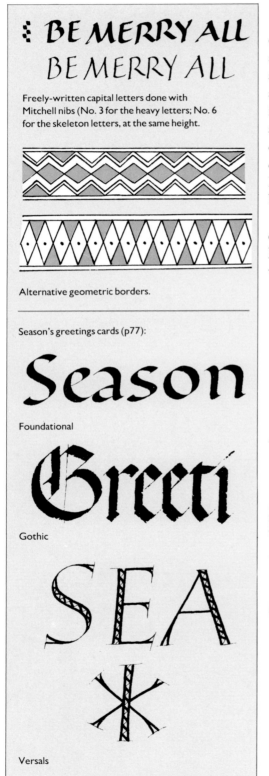

❖ BE MERRY ALL
BE MERRY ALL

Freely-written capital letters done with Mitchell nibs (No. 3 for the heavy letters; No. 6 for the skeleton letters, at the same height.

Alternative geometric borders.

Season's greetings cards (p77):

Season
Foundational

Greeti
Gothic

SEA
✳
Versals

GREETINGS CARDS are popular projects for both beginners and experienced calligraphers alike. Their ephemeral nature also encourages experiment with design and printing techniques, such as embossing, rubber stamps or letter rubbings. The main factors to take into account are: working on a small scale; creating a decorative impact; and deciding how to reproduce the card. Very simple cards, can be written by hand in large numbers quite easily, but an economical way of reproducing small quantities of a more complex design is by photocopying. If you want to reproduce larger quantities of cards, the best method is probably offset lithography, (*see p67*).

This Christmas card project can be photocopied and coloured by hand, or printed. Letter weight is varied by keeping the same letter height and changing the nibwidth. You will need: basic equipment (*see pp36-7*).

BE·MERRY·ALL·BE·MERRY·ALL
✳ WITH·HOLLY·DRESS·THE ✳
FESTIVE·HALL·PREPARE·THE
✳ SONG·THE·FEAST·THE·BALL✳
TO·WELCOME·MERRY·CHRISTMAS

a

BE MERRY ALL
✳ BE MERRY ALL
WITH HOLLY
DRESS THE
FESTIVE HALL
PREPARE THE
✳ SONG THE
FEAST THE BALL
TO WELCOME
✳ MERRY ✳
CHRISTMAS

b

1 Start by drawing some thumbnail sketches in pencil or pen, trying out different formats. In **a** and **b** the texture of a block of capitals is altered by separating the words with dots or stars. **c** Having decided on a format, move on to pen-written roughs and alternative layouts. **d** To add some variety to the block of capitals, italic lower-case letters were incorporated for some of the lines. **e** Changing the weight of the capital gives a more interesting variety of texture; several combinations were tried, with emphasis added to different parts. The lettering was written freely, using just a baseline, but beginners will find it easier to write between two lines.

BE MERRY ALL
BE MERRY ALL
WITH HOLLY
DRESS THE
FESTIVE HALL
PREPARE THE
SONG THE
FEAST THE BALL
TO WELCOME
MERRY
CHRISTMAS

c

Be merry all
✳ Be merry all
WITH HOLLY
✳ DRESS THE
FESTIVE HALL
Prepare the ✳
✳ song the
feast the ball
TO WELCOME
✳ MERRY ✳
CHRISTMAS

d

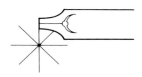

2 The fine lines of the stars are made by turning the pen for each stroke to use the narrow edge of the nib.

BE MERRY ALL
✳ BE MERRY ALL
WITH HOLLY ✳
✳ DRESS THE
FESTIVE HALL
PREPARE THE
SONG THE ✳
FEAST THE BALL
TO WELCOME
✳ MERRY ✳
CHRISTMAS

e

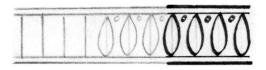

3 To contrast with the freedom of the letters, a geometric decorative border was designed (shown here at actual size) and colour added. First rule the two parallel horizontal lines in pencil, and then make the vertical divisions. Draw the curved shapes. Now rule the straight lines with technical drawing pens. Finally, draw the curved shapes with an edged nib. Work the border in one line and cut in half for a top and bottom border, or make a good photocopy for the second half. Clean up the edges with white gouache.

PAPER FOLDING

Clever use of paper folding means that you can print or photocopy one sheet of paper, but end up with text on more than one surface of the card. Make sure that you print on to firm paper, and that the grain runs down the fold so that the card stands without curling. Shading indicates the front of the card.

French fold Printing on one side of the sheet will appear on the inside and outside of the card.

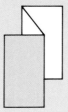

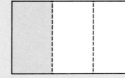

Z-fold Printing on one sheet folds to front, middle and inside back.

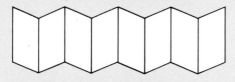

Concertina folding Make as many parallel folds as you want for a concertina effect.

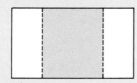

Shutter opening One printing gives text on the "windows", or alternatively, on the inside.

4 Write out the two different weights of text separately on layout paper, cut them out and then paste them in position on a sheet of ruled up cartridge paper. The line space is based on a fixed measurement, and then adjusted by eye. Stick down the borders last and indicate the margins with trim marks. When printed, add colour to the border by painting on a light wash of paint.

Actual size 150 × 95mm (6 × 3¾in).
Calligraphy by Patricia Gidney.

190mm (7½in)

150mm (5⅞in)

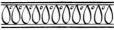

BE MERRY ALL
✳BE MERRY ALL
WITH HOLLY ✳
✳DRESS THE
FESTIVE HALL
PREPARE THE
SONG THE ✳
FEAST THE BALL
TO WELCOME
✳ MERRY ✳
CHRISTMAS

63mm (2½in)

95mm (3¾in)

fold mark   trim mark

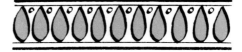

BE MERRY ALL
✳ BE MERRY ALL
WITH HOLLY ✳
✳ DRESS THE
FESTIVE HALL
PREPARE THE
SONG THE ✳
FEAST THE BALL
TO WELCOME
✳ MERRY ✳
CHRISTMAS

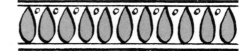

✳ SEASONS ✳
GREETINGS

seasons greetings

Seasons Greetings

Season's
Greetings

greetings

GREETINGS
GREETINGS
SEASON'S
GREETINGS
GREETINGS
GREETINGS
GREETINGS

These cards, displaying the same message, but
written in different scripts, illustrate the variety that
can be achieved, even with a very simple design. All
of the cards can be reproduced by photocopying or
printing, but the simpler ones could be written by
hand in large quantities. Top to bottom: versals,
uncials, gothic, foundational hand, italic and capitals.

77

INVITATION

Italic, before reduction, using Mitchell nibs.

Charlot

No. 2 nib

All Saints

No. 3 nib

AVENUE

No. 4 nib

Charlotte

All Saint

request the

Avenue

Copperplate, before reduction. The same pointed, flexible nib was used for all the writing: Gillot 404.

a e r
g n k
H E M

When writing guest names on the printed invitations, or when addressing the envelopes, add some simple flourishes, either for a decorative effect, or to correct any centring problems. You may find it easier to use a fountain pen.

THE traditional, centred arrangement of these printed invitations is ideal for a formal occasion; italic and copperplate are both suitable writing styles. You can prepare your work as a paste-up, which allows for perfect centring, and for correcting mistakes. Unless you are very confident at writing with small nibs, it is advisable to work at a larger size, and then to have your work reduced. Start by checking the wording, deciding on a format that will fit a standard envelope, and finding a printer. You will need: basic equipment (*see pp36-7*).

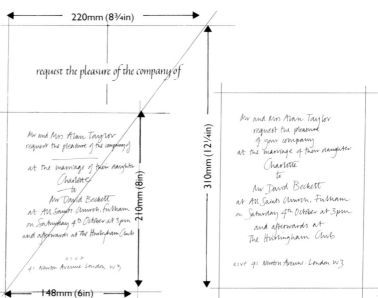

1 Using layout or cartridge paper, draw up the measurements of the invitation (smaller than the envelope!). Make some rough sketches in pen or pencil. Now scale up the invitation: any rectangle that has a corner on the diagonal line shown will be in proportion to the original. Working "half-up" gives a manageable size. Allowing generous margins, write out the longest line with a variety of nibs until you find a suitable one. Here a No. 3 nib was used, and an x-height of 5 nib-widths.

Mr and Mrs Allen Taylor
request the pleasure of the company of
at the marriage of their daughter
Charlotte to Mr David Beckett
at All Saints Church, Fulham
on Saturday 4th October at 3 pm
and afterwards at the Hurlingham Club
R S V P 41 Newton Avenue, London W 3
Mr and Mrs Allen Taylor The The
at All Saints Church, Fulham

R S V P 41 Newton Avenue London W 3

2 Now rule up a sheet of layout paper and write out all the text. Do not try to arrange it at this stage. Rewrite any lines that need to be corrected, and experiment with alternative nib sizes and letter weights. If possible, it is a good idea to take several photocopies – a couple at actual size in order to make alternative layouts, and one at the reduced size, to check that the writing and the design still work well when reduced for printing.

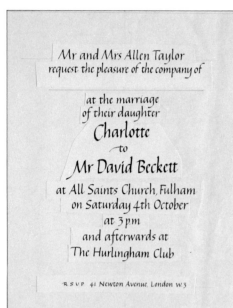

Mr and Mrs Allen Taylor
request the pleasure
of the company of

at the marriage of their daughter

Charlotte
to
Mr David Beckett

at All Saints Church, Fulham
on Saturday 4th October at 3 pm
and afterwards at the Hurlingham Club

R S V P 41 Newton Avenue, London W.3

Mr and Mrs Allen Taylor
request the pleasure of the company of

at the marriage
of their daughter
Charlotte
to
Mr David Beckett
at All Saints Church, Fulham
on Saturday 4th October
at 3 pm
and afterwards at
The Hurlingham Club

R S V P 41 Newton Avenue, London W.3

3 Rule out the area for the enlarged layout and then rule a central vertical line. Cut the lines of text into strips, fold them in half and centre them on the line (see pp66-7). Do several different layouts at this stage, varying the space between the lines and the length of the lines. Rewrite lines that seem to need a different emphasis, such as the names, or the address. Try a shorter x-height, or a wider nib, as shown.

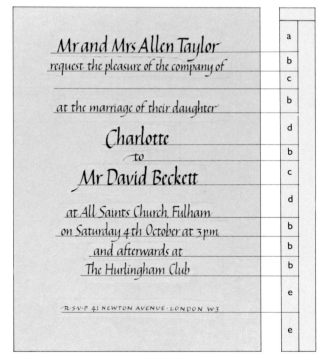

Mr and Mrs Allen Taylor
request the pleasure of the company of

at the marriage of their daughter
Charlotte
to
Mr David Beckett

at All Saints Church, Fulham
on Saturday 4th October at 3pm
and afterwards at
The Hurlingham Club

R·S·V·P 41 NEWTON AVENUE · LONDON W3

	a
	b
	c
	b
	d
	b
	c
	d
	b
	b
	b
	e
	e

4 A layout done by eye will need to be neatened up. Mark off the line spaces on a strip of paper. Standardize those that should be of the same measurement. Here, a = 40mm (1⅝in), b = 17mm (¾in), c = 20mm (⅞in), d = 30mm (1¼in), e = 35mm (1⅜in). Now transfer these measurements on to a piece of cartridge paper which has been ruled at the enlarged size. Stick the strips of text in position, and make any final spacing adjustments (line space is affected by the ascenders and descenders). Add trim marks, and an overlay with printing instructions.

GUESTS' NAMES

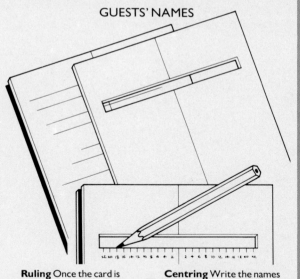

Ruling Once the card is printed, the names can be added in your own handwriting to contrast with the lettering, or in the same style as the invitation. A handy shortcut for ruling pencil lines involves cutting a card template, so that it aligns with the top of the invitation, and has an opening positioned at the width of the x-height for the letters. Place it on the invitation, and rule the lines.

Centring Write the names out first on a piece of paper, fold them in half and use them as a guide. Alternatively, add a scale to the template, indicating the number of letters (and spaces) in a name, marked from the centre outwards. This will only work if you have estimated an average from consistently spaced writing. This technique is also very useful for writing names on diplomas.

Copperplate "script" is a popular typeface for invitations, but a hand-written copperplate is much more distinctive. This invitation was done in a similar way to the italic invitation, written 50% larger than the size at which it is printed. When reducing by this amount, the thin strokes should be relatively heavy in the original, or they will break up on reduction. Names can be added at the top, or omitted.

The printer will reduce, print and fold your work. Any colour is possible, although black or grey on white is the traditional combination. Thermographic printing produces a shiny, raised surface, which imitates engraving. The paper should be heavy enough to stand up; a thin card is often used.

Italic invitation: printed size 210 × 148mm (8 × 6in)
Calligraphy by Susanne Haines
Copperplate invitation: printed size: 210 × 148mm (8 × 6in)
Calligraphy by Andrew Parkinson

Mr and Mrs Allen Taylor
request the pleasure of your company
at the marriage of their daughter

Charlotte
to
Mr David Beckett

at All Saints Church, Fulham
on Saturday 4th October at 3 p.m.

and afterwards at
The Hurlingham Club

· R.S.V.P. · 41 Newton Avenue · London · W3 ·

Mr and Mrs Allen Taylor
request the pleasure of your company
at the marriage of their daughter
Charlotte
to
Mr David Beckett

at All Saints Church, Fulham
on Saturday 4th October at 3 p.m.
and afterwards at
The Hurlingham Club

· R.S.V.P. · 41 Newton Avenue · London · W3 ·

Mr and Mrs Allen Taylor
request the pleasure of the company of
Mr Paul Holden
at the marriage of their daughter

Charlotte
to
Mr David Beckett

at All Saints Church, Fulham
on Saturday 4th October at 3 pm
and afterwards at
The Hurlingham Club

· R·S·V·P 41 NEWTON AVENUE · LONDON W3

Mr P. Holden
10 Cleveland Road
LONDON W3

WINE LABEL

A CALLIGRAPHIC label will add distinction to any wine! This project shows a method of designing a label for commercial use, and it also deals with two points: how to combine a black and white illustration with calligraphy in a way that achieves a balance in terms of weight and texture; and how to fit a considerable amount of information into a small area. The early stages were written without lines, roughly in position. With practice, you will find that it becomes easier to estimate spacing, suitable nib sizes and letter height. You need: basic equipment (*see pp36-7*), white scraperboard, scraper tool, a brush, and waterproof black Indian ink.

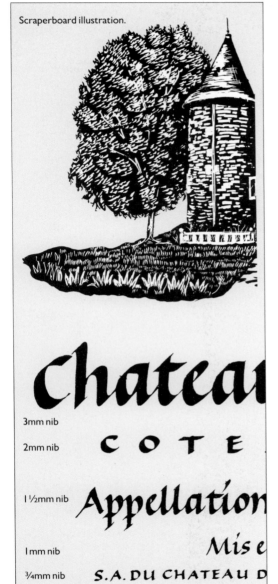

Scraperboard illustration.

3mm nib
2mm nib

1½mm nib

1mm nib
¾mm nib

1mm nib

2mm nib

Italic, foundational hand and Roman capitals were used in the design of the label, and are shown here before reduction. All the lettering was done with Brause nibs.

a

1 Make thumbnail sketches **a** at actual size. **b** Determine the emphasis needed for the various types of information. Least prominence was given to the proprietor's line, therefore it was written with the smallest manageable nib, using widely spaced capitals to vary the texture of the line. The length of this line dictated the working format. **c** A second rough increases the weight of the first two lines, giving them more emphasis.

b

Chateau d'Archignac
COTES DE BOURG

Appellation de Cotes de Bourg Controlée
Mis en bouteilles au Chateau
S.A. DU CHATEAU D'ARCHIGNAC · PROPRIÉTAIRE · H. LACHAIZE
shipped by
Eldridge, Pope and Co., Dorshester, Dorset, England

1979   e 70cl

c

Chateau d'Archignac
COTES DE BOURG

Appellation de Cotes de Bourg Controlée
Mise en bouteilles au Chateau
S.A. DU CHATEAU D'ARCHIGNAC · PROPRIÉTAIRE · H. LACHAIZE
Shipped by
Eldridge, Pope and Co., Dorchester, Dorset, England

SCRAPERBOARD

Work in proportion to the lettering. **a** Make a preliminary drawing. **b** Trace the drawing, and rub red conté crayon on the reverse side. Attach the tracing (right side up) to the scraperboard with tape and trace the outline. Flip up the tracing paper. **c** Brush in the outline. Replace the tracing and **d** trace the main details through. **e** Scratch the details in.

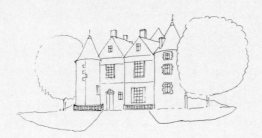

a

b

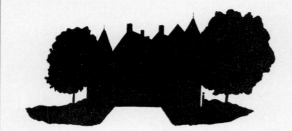

c

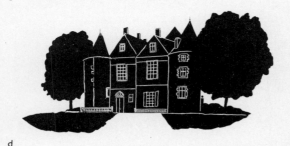

d

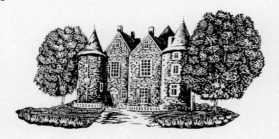

e

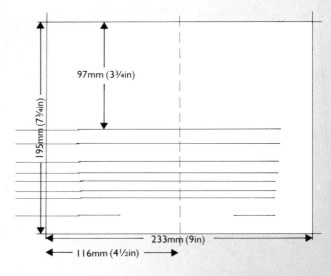

97mm (3¾in)

195mm (7¾in)

233mm (9in)

116mm (4½in)

2 Before finalizing the layout, make a reduced photocopy to actual size to see how the text and illustration work together. The black and white contrast of scraperboard illustration generally balances well with calligraphy. Such a large reduction tends to distort letters and spacing, also the fine strokes may disappear. Make final spacing adjustments. Rule for the paste-up.

Chateau d'Archignac
COTES DE BOURG
Appellation Côtes de Bourg Contrôlée
Mis en bouteilles au Chateau
S.A. DU CHATEAU D'ARCHIGNAC · PROPRIÉTAIRE H. LACHAIZE
Shipped by
Eldridge, Pope and Co., Dorchester, Dorset, England
1979   e70cl

3 Rule up and write the text on layout paper. Cut out the lines, fold them in half and centre the strips on the vertical line. The final paste-up and the scraperboard drawing should be reduced to size by PMT (*see pp66-7*). The scraperboard is quite thick, so a PMT is essential. (A good quality photocopy would be adequate for a non-commercial wine label.) In this case, the name of the wine did not reduce well, therefore it was rewritten at actual size (with a 2mm nib) and pasted on the finished artwork. Always make a final check for possible spelling mistakes. An error in the third line of this label was noticed at the final paste-up stage. Finally, stick the illustration in position, add the trim marks, and cover with an overlay.

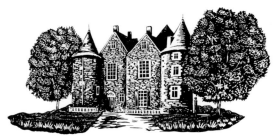

Chateau d'Archignac
COTES DE BOURG

Appellation Côtes de Bourg Contrôlée

Mis en bouteilles au Chateau

S.A. DU CHATEAU D'ARCHIGNAC · PROPRIÉTAIRE H. LACHAIZE

Shipped by
Eldridge, Pope and Co., Dorchester, Dorset, England

1979   **e70cl**

At this stage, a commercial wine label would either be passed back to the client for approval, or sent for printing on adhesive labels.

Reproduced at actual size.
Calligraphy and illustration by Gerald Fleuss.

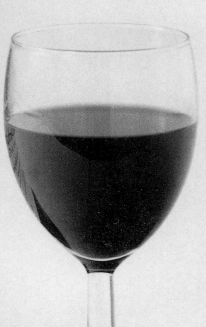

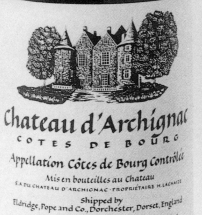

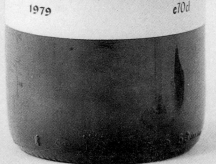

Labels for homemade wine or other produce, such as jams, can be prepared in a similar way. Such labels are not likely to include as much wording, so you can work at the actual size of the label. Photocopying the finished artwork is more economical than printing. Use a water-based adhesive to stick the labels to the bottles. Alternatively, photocopy several at a time on to self-adhesive labels (check the size of the labels before you start designing!). Decorative borders can be drawn with the pen, or you can use dry transfer borders.

PRINTED STATIONERY

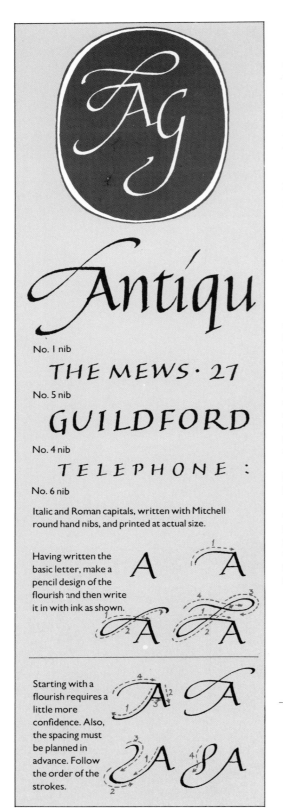

No. 1 nib

THE MEWS · 27

No. 5 nib

GUILDFORD

No. 4 nib

TELEPHONE :

No. 6 nib

Italic and Roman capitals, written with Mitchell round hand nibs, and printed at actual size.

Having written the basic letter, make a pencil design of the flourish and then write it in with ink as shown.

Starting with a flourish requires a little more confidence. Also, the spacing must be planned in advance. Follow the order of the strokes.

COMMERCIAL stationery should immediately convey the nature of a business, therefore the challenge is in designing an image and choosing a style of lettering that reflects the company's identity: for example, the writing style and the logo of this letterheading reflect the nature of the antiques business. You will need to consider how the design will look when combined with writing or typing, and what impression it will give to the receiver when it is removed from the envelope and unfolded. Also, should the compliment slip have space for messages; does the business card have to be a standard size? A personal letterheading is probably more fun to do, because it can be less restrictive to design. You will need: basic equipment (*see pp36-7*).

1 The arrangement of the text and the design of the logo must complement each other. In this design the dominant shape of the logo was determined first, and italic was chosen as a suitable style for the company name. The flourished capitals of the logo are reflected in the flourish of the "A".

Alternatives for the logo were tried, with the letters on different levels.

To construct an oval, draw one quarter of the shape on a piece of tracing paper, fold in half twice (once in each direction) and trace the rest of the shape through.

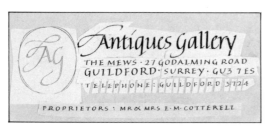

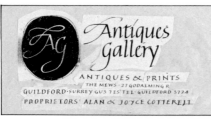

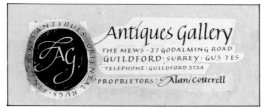

2 Try out paste-ups of various arrangements of the text, with the letters at different heights and weights. Here, the paper size is A4 (210 × 297mm/8 × 11in). The company name is written in a rounded italic with a No. 1 nib. Small Roman capitals (No. 5 nib) for the address give a contrast of weight, and writing the town and telephone at different sizes (Nos. 4 and 6) adds some variety. The photocopied final rough for the letterheading (right) shows the proprietors' names placed at the bottom of the sheet, in white on black, to balance the weight of the logo.

DESIGNING THE LOGO

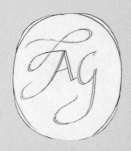

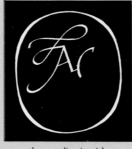

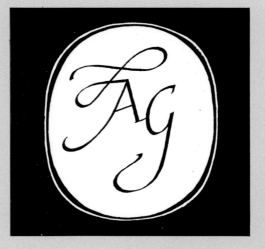

Trace the design on to a piece of black paper, then outline it with a white crayon. Use white gouache and a No. 4 nib to write the letters. Paint the border with a fine sable brush, making visual adjustments to the shape if necessary. Finally, cut carefully around the border, leaving a thin black outline. Alternatively (right), design the logo in black on white and ask the printer to reverse it photographically. To retain the black outline, paint a black border.

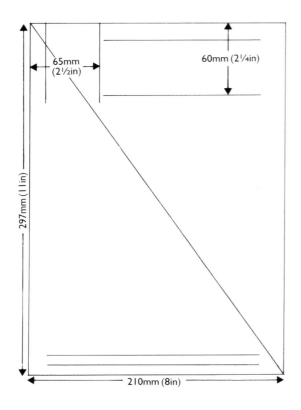

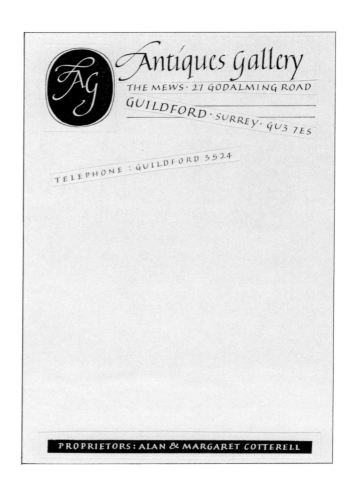

3 To prepare for the final paste-up: mark out an area for an A4 (210 × 297mm/8 × 11in) letterheading on a piece of board or heavy cartridge paper, transfer the measurements from the final rough and rule up. Rewrite, or assemble existing strips of text, on layout paper and glue them in place with rubber cement. Draw trim marks in place and then cover the paste-up with an overlay of tracing paper or layout paper.

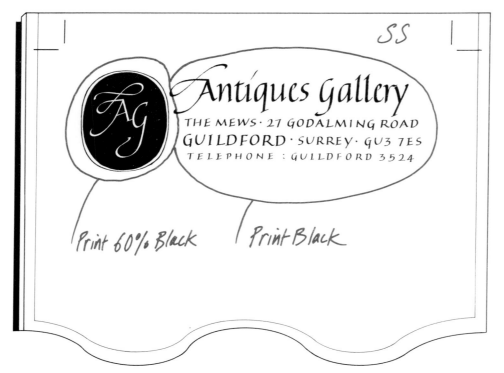

4 If you require part of the design printed in another colour, this should be marked on the overlay. Remember that printing in another colour will change the weight and emphasis of the writing, so try a rough of its final appearance with paint.

Printing in two colours is done in two stages and is therefore more expensive. In this case, where black and grey are used, there is an alternative method of printing which will give the effect of grey. The instruction should read, "print 60% black", or whatever percentage tint you require (*see pp66-7*).

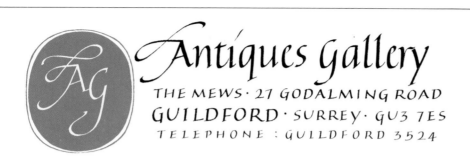

The full printed set of stationery shows how the letterheading has been adapted. For the compliments slip (which is one third the size of the letter), it was a simple matter of adding the wording written at the same size as the first line of the address. The design was further adapted for the business card (which is the size of a standard credit card). The text was rearranged within an enlarged format at the same proportion to the card (*see pp66-7*), and then reduced by the printer.

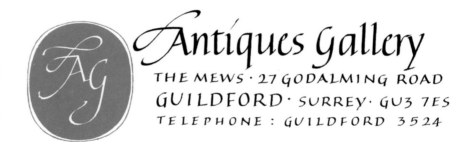

PROPRIETORS: ALAN & MARGARET COTTERELL

Actual size of letterheading: A4 (210 × 297mm/8 × 11in); compliments slip: 210 × 100mm (8¼ × 4in); business card 170 × 95mm (6½ × 3¾in). Calligraphy by Gaynor Goffe.

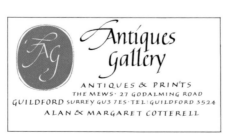

CALENDAR

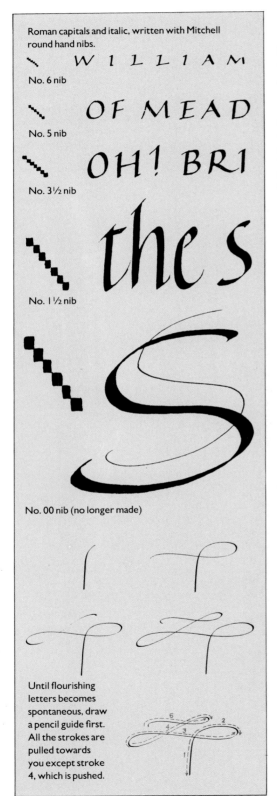

Roman capitals and italic, written with Mitchell round hand nibs.

WILLIAM

No. 6 nib

OF MEAD

No. 5 nib

OH! BRI

No. 3½ nib

the s

No. 1½ nib

S

No. 00 nib (no longer made)

Until flourishing letters becomes spontaneous, draw a pencil guide first. All the strokes are pulled towards you except stroke 4, which is pushed.

CALENDAR design can be approached in many ways: an image for the whole year, or a page for each month; texts with a linking theme, or expressive lettering, to name but a few. For this project a quotation was chosen to capture the spirit of each month.

To create a personal visual interpretation of a text, start by reading the words over and over again, until they begin to suggest what should be emphasized, and how it should be evoked. Think of the calendar working as a whole, and aim either for continuity, or for contrast. You will need: basic equipment (*see pp36-7*).

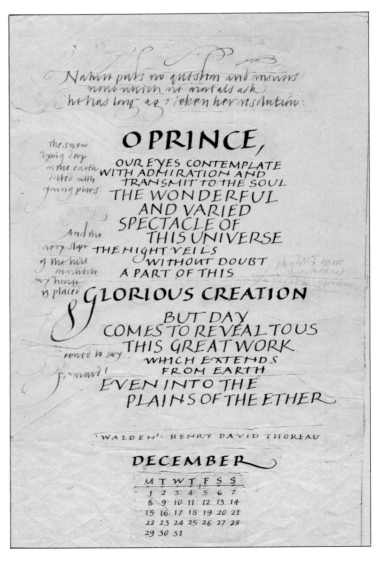

I This rough design explores the textural variation of capital letters at different weights and heights.

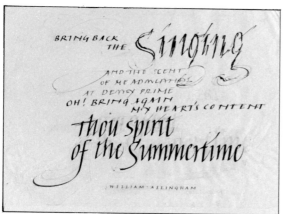

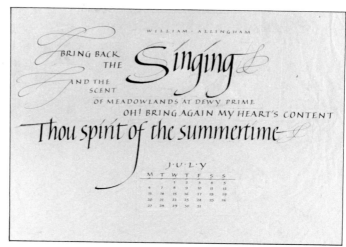

2 Start with rough designs for all the months. The first rough for July was made with edged pens, and determined the general arrangement and emphasis. "Singing" is freely written with double-stroke letters and "Thou spirit of the summertime" is quickly written with an angular form.

In this alternative landscape format, "singing" is written with the more normal italic form for "g".

3 This second rough shows a paste-up of the design in a portrait format. The word "singing" is now written with solid letters, and "Thou spirit of the summertime" is written more carefully, with less angular forms. The capital letters are formed more accurately, while retaining the freedom of the rough. (It is easy to lose the spontaneity of letter forms as the work progresses.) The flourishes are kept light by writing them with a thinner pen than the letters themselves. At this point the final text was written out, and the line spacing was transferred to a piece of board, which was then ruled up for a paste-up and prepared for printing at a reduced size.

Once all the months have been designed, the pages can be printed, backed with cardboard and bound. A cheaper alternative is to photocopy the calendar on to heavy paper or card of any colour, and punch a hole at the top.

Actual size: 297 × 210mm (11½ × 8¼in)
Calligraphy by Gaynor Goffe.

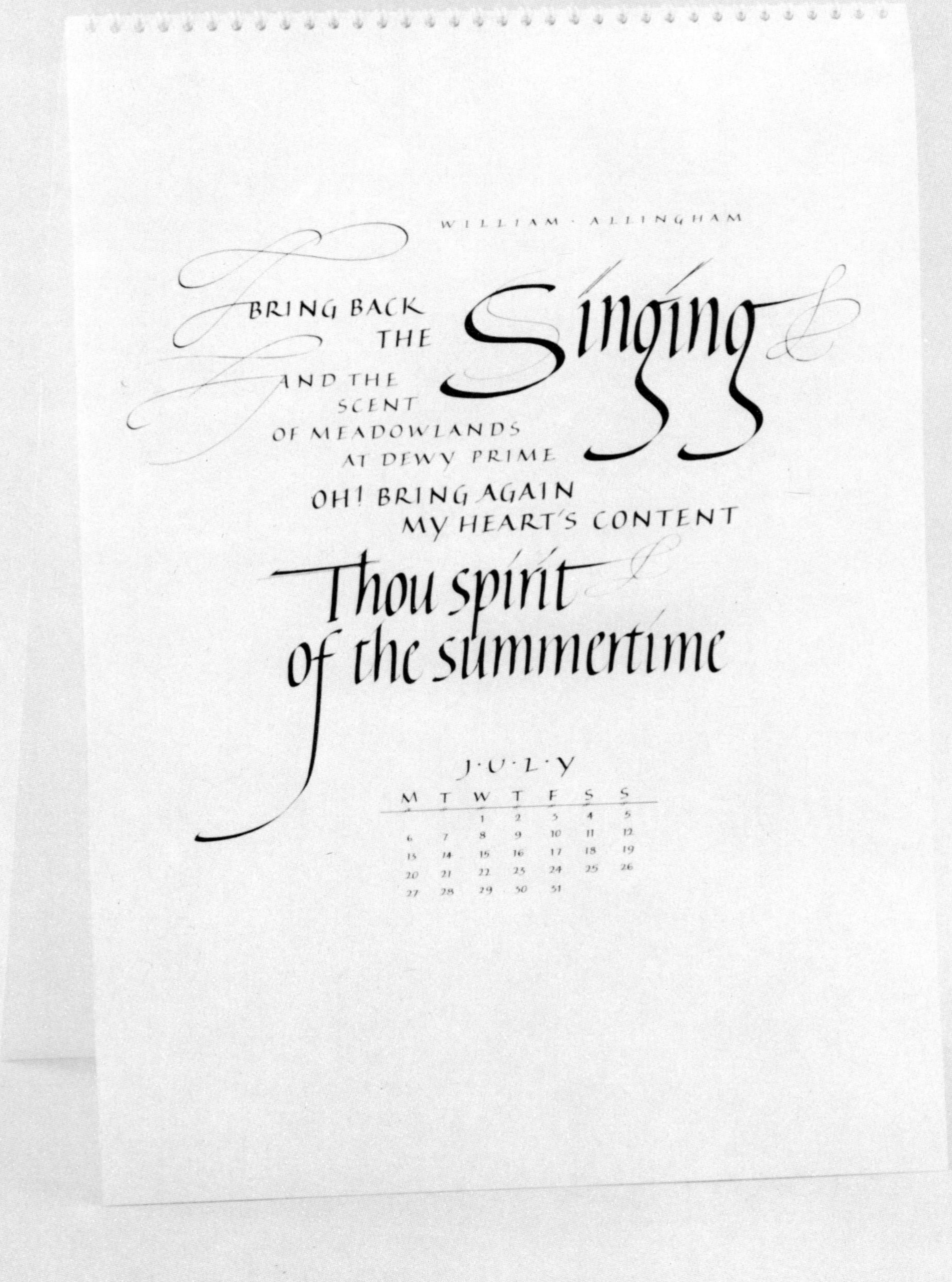

WILLIAM · ALLINGHAM

BRING BACK
THE *Singing*
AND THE
SCENT
OF MEADOWLANDS
AT DEWY PRIME

OH! BRING AGAIN
MY HEART'S CONTENT

*Thou spirit
of the summertime*

J·U·L·Y

M	T	W	T	F	S	S
		1	2	3	4	5
6	7	8	9	10	11	12
13	14	15	16	17	18	19
20	21	22	23	24	25	26
27	28	29	30	31		

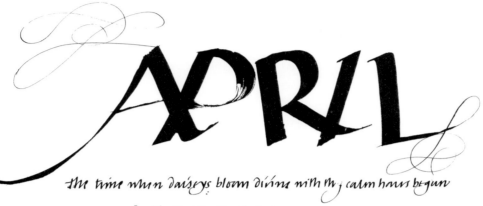

APRIL

the time when daiseys bloom divine with the calm hours begun

S	M	T	W	T	F	S	S	M	T	W	T	F	S
			1	2	3	4	5	6	7	8	9	10	11
12	13	14	15	16	17	18	19	20	21	22	23	24	25
26	27	28	29	30									

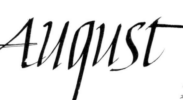

S	M	T	W	T	F	S
						1
2	3	4	5	6	7	8
9	10	11	12	13	14	15

The barley's beard is grey

August

JOHN·CLARE

and wheat is brown

S	M	T	W	T	F	S
16	17	18	19	20	21	22
23	24	25	26	27	28	29
30	31					

S	M	T	W	T	F	S	S	M	T	W	T	F	S
		1	2	3	4	5	6	7	8	9	10	11	12

DECEMBER

13	14	15	16	17	18	19	20	21	22	23	24	25	26
27	28	29	30	31									

Christmas is come and every hearth makes room to give him welcome now

JOHN·CLARE

These early roughs have a totally different approach – an expressive
interpretation of the months, freely arranged within a landscape format.

MANUSCRIPT RIDDLE BOOK

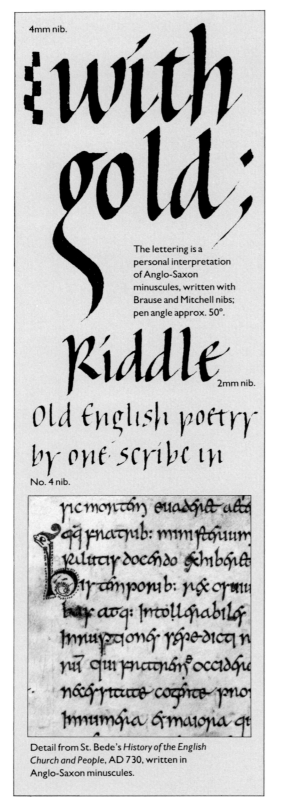

The lettering is a personal interpretation of Anglo-Saxon minuscules, written with Brause and Mitchell nibs; pen angle approx. 50°.

2mm nib.

No. 4 nib.

Detail from St. Bede's *History of the English Church and People*, AD 730, written in Anglo-Saxon minuscules.

THIS unusual manuscript book shows an inspired alternative approach to a traditional and popular calligraphic form: the unfolding of its binding creates a sense of suspense, while the arrangement of the text and margins is intuitive, rather than mathematically devised. Nonetheless, it is based on a simple design for a single-section sewn book.

The text is a translation of an 8th century Anglo-Saxon riddle, thus the choice of script suggested itself, just as the form of the piece was suggested by the answer to the riddle: "I am a book".

You will need: basic equipment (*see pp36-7*), text and cover paper (*see pp95-6*), gouache paints (madder carmine and burnt umber), needle and thread, and a small feather.

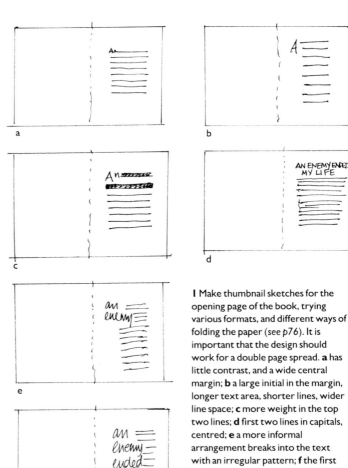

1 Make thumbnail sketches for the opening page of the book, trying various formats, and different ways of folding the paper (*see p76*). It is important that the design should work for a double page spread. **a** has little contrast, and a wide central margin; **b** a large initial in the margin, longer text area, shorter lines, wider line space; **c** more weight in the top two lines; **d** first two lines in capitals, centred; **e** a more informal arrangement breaks into the text with an irregular pattern; **f** the first phrase dominates.

2 Now develop the chosen thumbnail sketch into a rough at actual size. **a** A felt-pen rough soon determined the general arrangement of the first page, which then set the pattern for the rest of the pages. The design has a strong vertical emphasis, starting with the shape of the letters, and carrying through into the two thin shapes made by the two different weights of text, and the ample top and bottom margins. The extent of the book should now be worked out: either by making a rough mathematical estimation, or by quickly writing out the whole text.

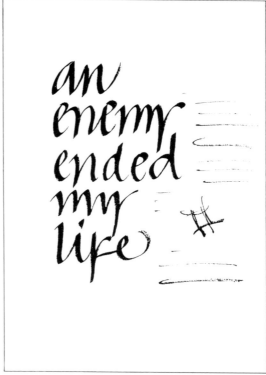

a

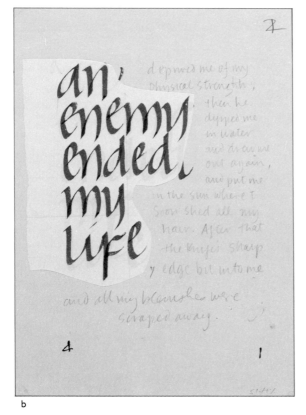

b

3 b In pencil, work out the fall of the text on the pages. The scale of the introductory phrase was echoed on subsequent pages by repeating phrases from the running text. Working with felt pen and paste-up for the phrases meant that layout was quicker, and more flexible. This stage required a considerable amount of planning —these selected phrases had to harmonize, both in terms of sense and design (*see p96*). The text was then written with a narrow edged pen **c**, which lost the contrast of scale and weight. As a result, it took numerous experiments with a variety of weights, papers, and colours before a balance was achieved between the texts, and also between the pages of a spread.

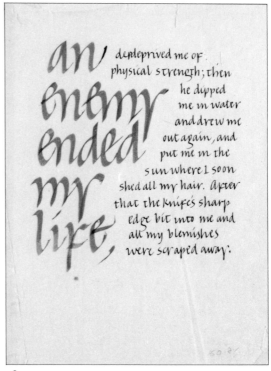

c

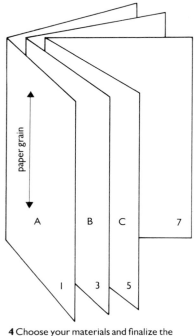

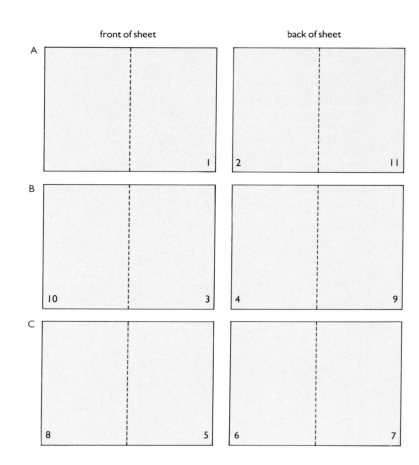

front of sheet   back of sheet

A

| 1 | 2 | 11 |

B

| 10 | 3 | 4 | 9 |

C

| 8 | 5 | 6 | 7 |

4 Choose your materials and finalize the fall of the text on the pages. Make up a "dummy" of your book by cutting out pages, and then folding and numbering them as shown. You can now work out the position of the writing: for instance, the last page and page 1 will be on one side of sheet "A"; while pages 2 and 11 will be on the other side.

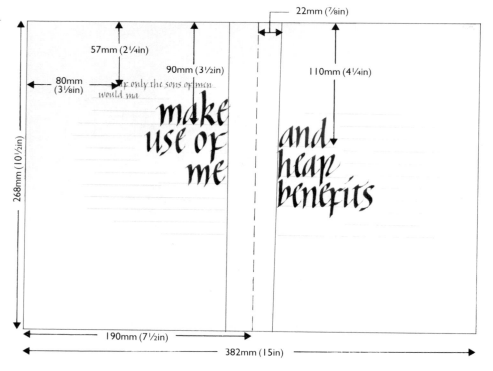

22mm (⅞in)

57mm (2¼in)

90mm (3½in)

80mm (3⅛in)

110mm (4¼in)

268mm (10½in)

190mm (7½in)

382mm (15in)

5 Mark out the pages, and cut to size, taking the paper grain into account (see p43). The measurements given are for the actual page size, as the paper was torn against a ruler for a ragged edge. Allow an extra margin if you want to trim the pages once the book has been sewn.

Mark the order of pages (see above) in pencil and rule up. The key measurements given for pages 6-7 can be used as a guide. Baselines only are ruled to allow for freedom in writing; line spacing is adjusted visually to allow for the ascenders and descenders. The constant measurements are the unusually narrow inner margins; the outer margins are visually equal. For a more conventional book, establish a constant top margin.

The large phrases should be written first, and then the small text (see p96). Work on one side of all the sheets first.

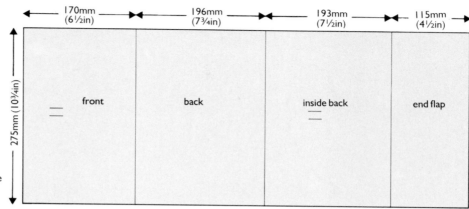

170mm (6½in)	196mm (7¾in)	193mm (7½in)	115mm (4½in)
front	back	inside back	end flap

275mm (10¾in)

6 The cover of the book is a riddle in itself: made from a piece of heavy textured dark brown paper (Fabriano Roma), it envelops the book with a double fold, and is closed by a hasp made from a feather!

To make the cover, cut a piece of heavy paper slightly wider than the book size and crease down the folds. Close the cover and slip a piece of cardboard inside, beneath the "inside back". With a sharp blade, make two 13mm (½in) parallel cuts. Remove the cardboard.

Now sew the book into the cover. A thick brown silk thread was used here.

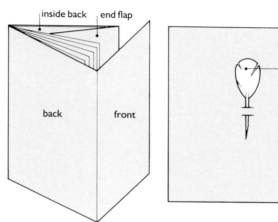

inside back   end flap

back   front

7 The cover is closed by threading a small feather through the cuts. This design creates a degree of suspense as it unfolds; the "end flap" covers only half of the title page, leaving the words revealed.

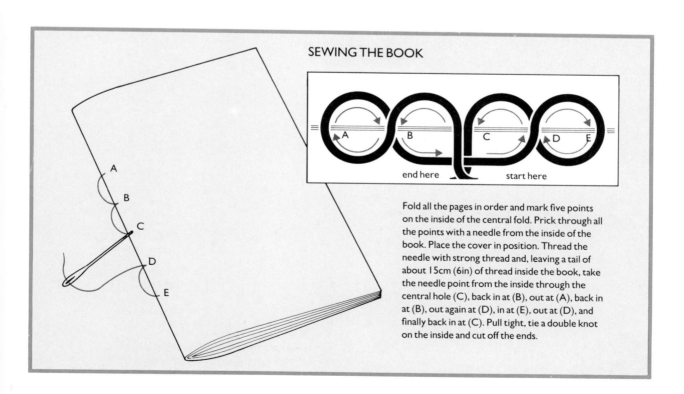

SEWING THE BOOK

end here   start here

A   B   C   D   E

Fold all the pages in order and mark five points on the inside of the central fold. Prick through all the points with a needle from the inside of the book. Place the cover in position. Thread the needle with strong thread and, leaving a tail of about 15cm (6in) of thread inside the book, take the needle point from the inside through the central hole (C), back in at (B), out at (A), back in at (B), out again at (D), in at (E), out at (D), and finally back in at (C). Pull tight, tie a double knot on the inside and cut off the ends.

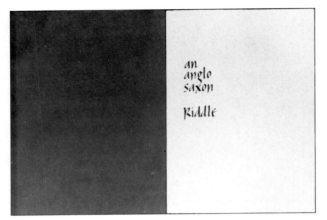

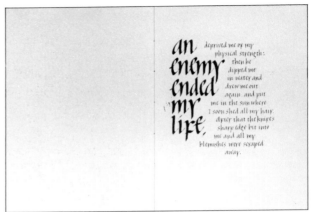

an
anglo
saxon

Riddle

an
enemy
ended
my
life,
deprived me of my
physical strength:
then he
dipped me
in water and
drew me out
again, and put
me in the sun where
I soon shed all my hair.
After that the knife's
sharp edge bit into
me and all my
blemishes were scraped
away.

Fingers folded me and
the birds feather often moved
over my
brown
surface,
sprinkling
meaningful
marks; it
swallowed more wood-dye
(part of the stream)
and again travelled over me
leaving black tracks. Then
a man bound me, he stretched
skin over me, adorned me
with gold;

Fingers
folded
me

and
adorned
me
with
gold;

thus I am
enriched by
the
wondrous
work
of smiths, wound
about with shining
metal. Now my
clasp and red
dye and these
glorious adornments
bring fame far
and wide to the
Protector of Men and
not to the pains of hell.

If only the sons of men
would make use
of me they
would be safer
and the more
victorious,
their hearts
would be bolder, their
minds more at ease,
their thoughts wiser; and
they would have more friends,
companions and
kinsmen

make
use of
me

Courageous,
honorable,
trusty and kind:
who would gladly
increase their
honour and
prosperity
and heap
benefits
upon them, ever
hold them most dear.

and
heap
benefits

ask
what
I am
called,

of such
service to
men. My name
is famous,
of service to
men and
sacred
in itself.

answer:
I am
a Book

Riddle 26 from Exeter Riddle Book
translated by Kevin Crossley-Holland.
The Anglo-Saxons loved sophisticated
riddles. The Exeter Riddle Book,
which contains a total of 96 riddles,
forms part of an anthology of
Old English poetry, probably copied
by one scribe in the last years of
the 10th century. The volume was
bequeathed to the Cathedral
Library by the first Bishop of Exeter,
Leofric, who died in 1072.

calligraphy based on a variety of
manuscripts from anglo-saxon times.
Lilly Lee Adamson January 1987

8 The design of the book should be conceived as a whole. The
irregular margins and the varied arrangement of the two weights of
lettering give an interesting pattern from page to page, as well as
providing a visual balance. The weight of the lettering in the title
page is echoed in the page with the answer.

A textured, cream-coloured mouldmade paper was used. The red
writing was done with madder carmine, the brown with burnt
umber. Adding a drop of gum arabic will prevent the paint from
rubbing off on the opposite page.

Fingers folded me and the bird's feather often moved over my **Fingers folded me** brown surface, sprinkling meaningful marks; it swallowed more wood-dye (part of the stream) and again travelled over me leaving black tracks. Then a man bound me, he stretched skin over me adorned me with gold;

and adorned me with gold; thus I am enriched by the wondrous work of smiths, wound about with shining metal. Now my clasp and red dye and these glorious adornments bring fame far and wide to the Protector of Men and not to the pains of hell.

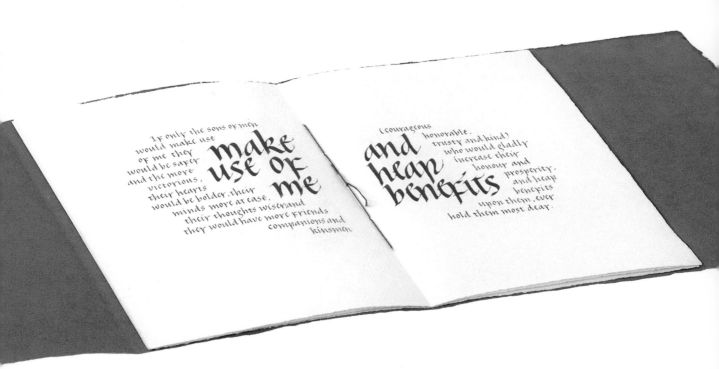

If only the sons of men would **make use of me** they would be safer and the more victorious, their hearts would be bolder, their minds more at ease, their thoughts wiser and they would have more friends companions and kinsmen

(courageous **and heap benefits** honorable, trusty and kind) who would gladly increase their honour and prosperity, and heap benefits upon them, ever hold them most dear.

Actual size of double page: 26.8 × 38.2 cm (10½ × 15in).
Calligraphy by Lilly Lee.
From 'The Exeter Book of Riddles' © translated by Kevin Crossley-Holland 1965,
1970 & 1978. Used by permission.

ILLUMINATION

You can learn a great deal about the use of colour and gold from studying historical examples. The illuminated panel and heraldry projects on the following pages demonstrate some of the traditional techniques, while the manuscript book (*p97*) and the garden plan (*see pp108-111*) illustrate a different use of colour, which, together with the examples in the first section of the book, show just some of the contemporary approaches to the art of illumination.

Colour is affected, not only by your own personal response to it (associations of mood, warmth, memory), but also by physical factors –light, adjacent colours, the colour and texture of the paper, and the quality of the paint. There is also the tonal quality of colour to consider (yellow, for instance, has a much lighter tone than black), and this will affect the weight of your writing.

Developing a sensitivity towards colour is important if you want to use it successfully. It is worth learning something about colour theory and colour mixing. Start with a limited range of colours (*see pp40-1*) and see what variety you can get from mixing them, before buying any ready-mixed shades and hues.

Colour preferences, and attitudes to the appropriateness of colour depend a great deal on taste. However, it is generally good advice to limit your palette and to aim for a harmonious colour range: for even within one part of the spectrum there is a vast number of possibilities: "There is flame red, blood red and rose red..." (Emil Nolde).

If work you are doing involves both colour and gilding, gild first, otherwise the gold will adhere to the medium in the paint and cover it.

Gilding does not have to involve very specialized techniques: two simple methods are shown. You can also use gold gouache from tubes; gold ink which is sold in bottles, tends to separate and is difficult to handle; there are even gold felt pens which can be used for greetings cards and other more ephemeral work.

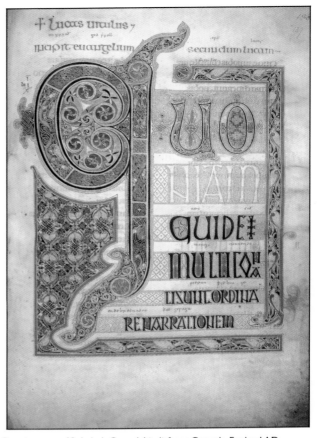

Opening page of St Luke's Gospel, Lindisfarne Gospels, England AD 698. Actual size of page: 340 × 250mm (13 × 10in).
The rich colours of this magnificent manuscript are intensified by the use of outlining, which prevents each colour from mixing visually with its neighbours.

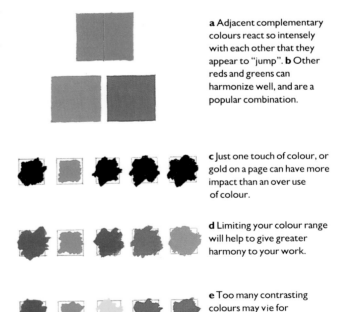

a Adjacent complementary colours react so intensely with each other that they appear to "jump". **b** Other reds and greens can harmonize well, and are a popular combination.

c Just one touch of colour, or gold on a page can have more impact than an over use of colour.

d Limiting your colour range will help to give greater harmony to your work.

e Too many contrasting colours may vie for dominance, making tonal values difficult to control, and fragmenting the design.

PVA and transfer leaf PVA is a very convenient size (base) for gilding, and transfer leaf (which is backed with paper) is much easier to handle than loose leaf gold. **1** Outline the letter with a pen, using diluted PVA mixed with a little gouache. Decorated initials can be drawn with ink as the letter is outlined later in black. **2** Flood PVA into the whole letter with a brush. Allow the PVA to dry. This will take from 20 minutes to an hour, depending on the temperature and atmosphere of the room. **3** Breathe on the PVA a few times to reactivate the adhesion. Place the gold in position and press down with your thumb over a manageable area. Inspect the letter, breathe again over ungilded areas and then press the gold into these places. **4** When the whole letter is covered, use a small piece of silk to gently burnish the surface.

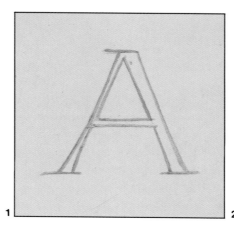

1

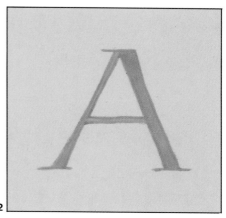

2

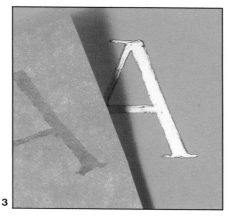

3

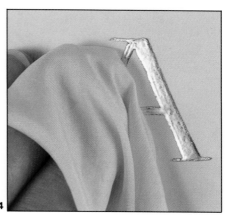

4

Shell gold is sold in powder form or in small tablets, and can be used in a similar way to paint (but with more care – it is very expensive!). **1** Draw the outline with a pen. **2** An undercoat of a suitable colour, such as yellow ochre, can be painted on to give extra body to the gold. Paint the gold on evenly with a short-haired sable brush. Use distilled water stored in a small airtight jar so that the gold fragments can be recycled. **3** When dry, polish up the gold. Begin by rubbing very gently with an agate burnisher, either directly on to the gold, or through a piece of crystal parchment if you prefer, and then increase the pressure. **4** Lines and dots can be scored into the surface of the gold to give a decorative pattern which will catch the light.

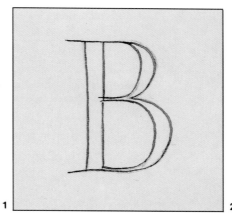

1

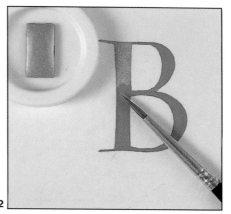

2

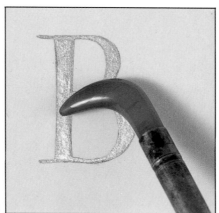

3

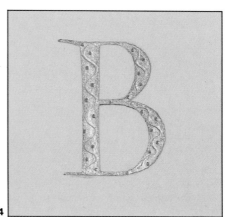

4

ILLUMINATED PANEL

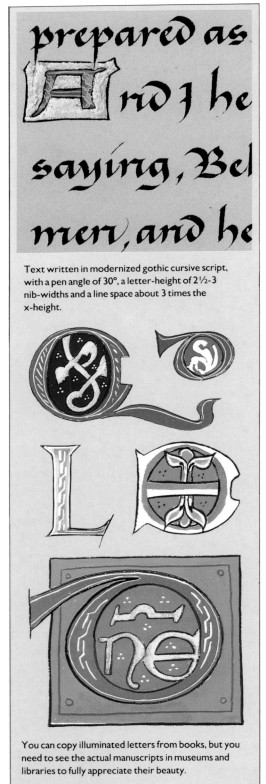

Text written in modernized gothic cursive script, with a pen angle of 30°, a letter-height of 2½-3 nib-widths and a line space about 3 times the x-height.

You can copy illuminated letters from books, but you need to see the actual manuscripts in museums and libraries to fully appreciate their beauty.

THIS project explains one of the ways you can achieve an elaborate style of decoration, by using a simple gilding technique, and by breaking it down into easy-to-follow steps. Once you are familiar with the working methods, you can try applying them to a modernized design. You will need: basic equipment (*see pp36-7*), a flexible pointed pen, waterproof ink, gouache (white, black, cobalt blue and carmine red), fine sable brushes (00, 1, 2), distilled water, PVA, transfer gold, a small piece of silk, and good handmade paper.

nd I saw a new heaven and a new earth: for the first heaven and the first earth were passed away; and there was no more sea. nd I John saw the holy city, new Jerusalem, coming down from God out of heaven, prepared as a bride adorned for her husband. nd I heard a great voice out of heaven saying, Behold, the tabernacle of God is with men, and he will dwell with them, and they shall be his people, and God himself shall be with them, and be their God. nd God shall wipe away all tears from their eyes; and there shall be no more death, neither sorrow, nor crying, neither shall there be any more pain; for the former things are passed away.

1 First, work out the overall design of the page. The elaborate initial letter must balance with the rest of the text, and should fit into the grid of writing lines (e.g this letter occupies five lines). Also, the margins should balance with the text area. Several roughs were done before the stage shown here. The margins are defined (*see p103*), the lines for the text ruled, the area occupied by the decorated letters marked in pencil, and the text written.

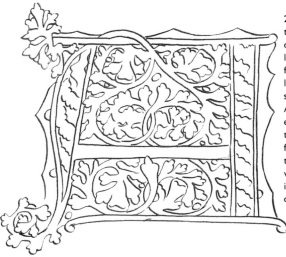

2 Define the details of the letter and trace it on to the paper. This letter can be traced from the finished letter shown at actual size (opposite). Alternatively, make an enlarged photocopy of this letter and trace from it, having rubbed the back of the tracing with soft pencil. Draw in or trace the smaller decorated letters.

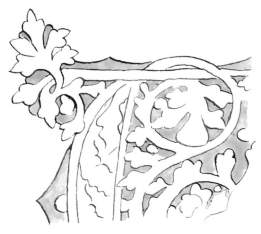

3 Start working on the large initial. Go over the outline with diluted waterproof ink, using a flexible pointed pen. When the ink is dry, rub out the pencil line with a soft eraser.

The gilding is done first. Mix up a small quantity of PVA with an equal amount of water, and a hint of gouache (enough to colour it). Brush it thinly on the areas to be gilded (the background here).

4 Allow the PVA to dry. Then moisten it slightly by breathing on it and apply the transfer gold, covering about 2 sq cm (1 sq in) at a time. To burnish, rub gently with a piece of silk (*see also pp98-9*).

Start the painting with a thin foundation layer of watered-down paint of both colours over the whole area. Allow it to dry.

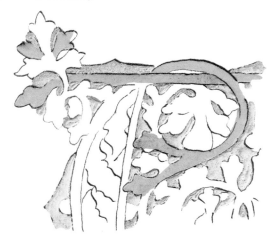

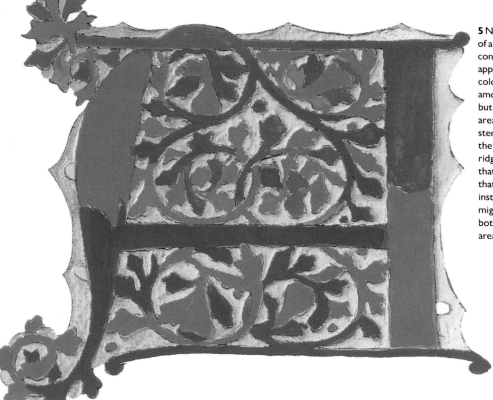

5 Now apply a second paint layer of a fairly thick, creamy consistency. At this stage you are applying the mid-tones of both colours (made by adding a small amount of white). Work quickly but surely when covering large areas, such as the crossbar and stems of the letter. Do not allow the paint to dry as you work, or ridges will form. Work in a way that is comfortable for you, and that will avoid smudging. For instance, a right-handed person might work from top left to bottom right. Protect the text areas with a piece of paper.

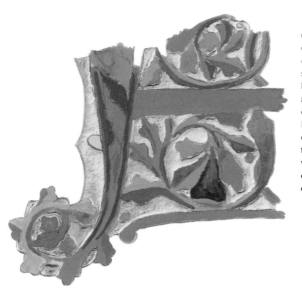

6 Now begin to add the light and dark tones. Work with one colour at a time. Start by mixing some more white with one of the base colours and add the light areas. Then use the pure base colour and add the dark tones. Repeat this with the other base colour. You may prefer to work from top to bottom, adding the various lights and darks as they occur. It is important to keep the different tones distinct.

7 Once all the colour has been applied, allow it to dry and then add the white highlight lines and dots. This will define and liven up the different areas of tone.

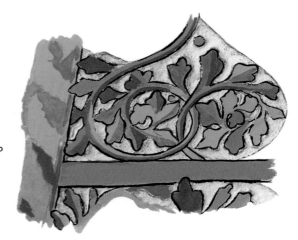

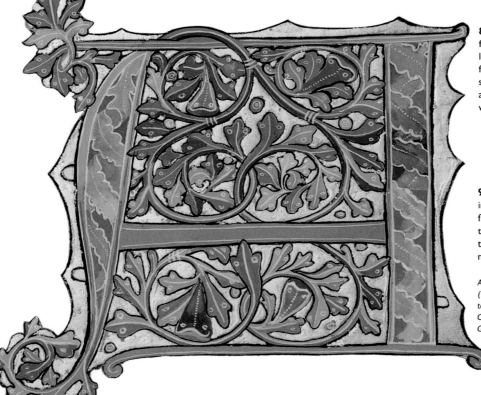

8 The final step is the addition of a fine, black outline. Be bold, and use a long-haired brush (00 or 1) for long, fluent brushstrokes. This outlining separates the different areas of tone and thus heightens the contrast, as well as sharpening up the details.

9 The small initial letters are worked in the same way. Gild all the letters first, and then add the colour. Finally, trim the paper. If you intend to frame the piece be sure that the glass does not touch the work.

*Actual size: margins 345 × 476mm
(13½ × 18¾in)
text area 310 × 230mm (9 × 12in)
Calligraphy and illumination by
Gerald Fleuss.*

And I saw a new heaven and a new earth: for the first heaven and the first earth were passed away; and there was no more sea. And I John saw the holy city, new Jerusalem, coming down from God out of heaven, prepared as a bride adorned for her husband. And I heard a great voice out of heaven saying, Behold, the tabernacle of God is with men, and he will dwell with them, and they shall be his people, and God himself shall be with them, and be their God. And God shall wipe away all tears from their eyes; and there shall be no more death, neither sorrow, nor crying, neither shall there be any more pain: for the former things are passed away.

HERALDRY

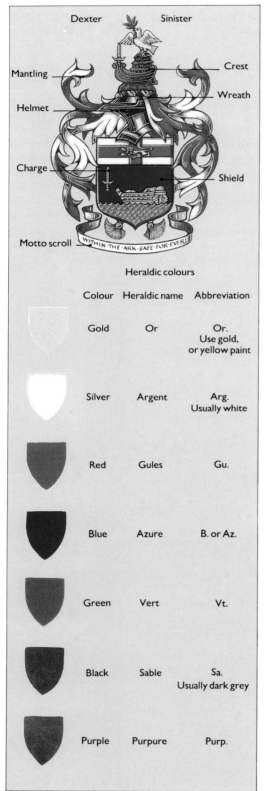

Dexter / Sinister

Mantling — Crest — Wreath

Helmet

Charge — Shield

Motto scroll — WITHIN·THE·ARK·SAFE·FOR·EVER

Heraldic colours

Colour	Heraldic name	Abbreviation
Gold	Or	Or. Use gold, or yellow paint
Silver	Argent	Arg. Usually white
Red	Gules	Gu.
Blue	Azure	B. or Az.
Green	Vert	Vt.
Black	Sable	Sa. Usually dark grey
Purple	Purpure	Purp.

HERALDRY developed in Western Europe in medi-aeval times, basically as a method of identi-fication, and is still in wide practical use today. It is often combined with calligraphy, for formal commemorative addresses, family trees, and on occasions when a coat of arms is an important part of the design.

The planning and painting of a civic "achievement", or armorial bearings, will introduce you to some of the terms and conventions used in heraldry, and also point to the variety of design possibilities. You will need: basic equipment (*see pp36-7*), paint (*see p106*), shell gold, Chinese stick ink, sable brushes, prepared vellum, or good quality handmade paper.

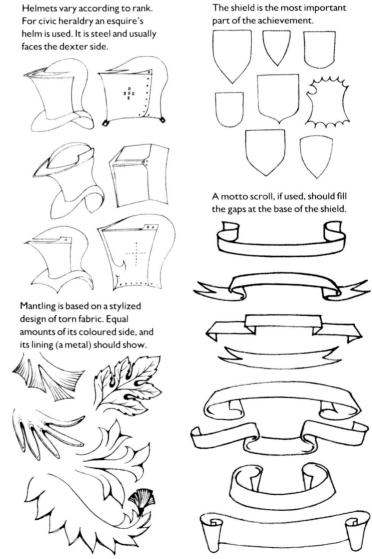

Helmets vary according to rank. For civic heraldry an esquire's helm is used. It is steel and usually faces the dexter side.

The shield is the most important part of the achievement.

A motto scroll, if used, should fill the gaps at the base of the shield.

Mantling is based on a stylized design of torn fabric. Equal amounts of its coloured side, and its lining (a metal) should show.

1 The blazon defines what must be included in an achievement. However, the overall shape of the design, and the stylistic treatment are in the hands of the heraldic artist.

Read the blazon carefully, and then assemble the parts, choosing shapes that will combine well. Contain sketches of the overall design within a suitable shape —square, oval or rectangular – to give it cohesion. Much of the drawing is symmetrical, thus you can draw one half, fold it vertically, and trace the other half. Paint in the colour roughly to check that it balances visually. Shading is governed by the convention that light should fall from the top left.

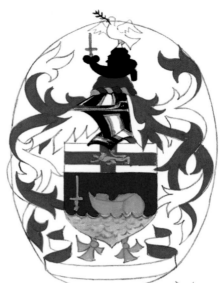

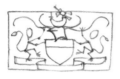

BLAZON

Azure in a sea proper the hull of a ship or, and for difference in the dexter chief point a sword erect point upwards of the last, on a chief argent a cross gules charged with a lion passant guardant or.
Crest: Upon a wreath of the colours on an ark sable resting upon a mount vert a dove bearing an olive branch proper, and for difference in the prow of the ark a sword as in the arms.
Mantling: Gules doubled argent.
Motto: Within the ark safe for ever.

Key: *proper* natural; *dexter* right (as viewed from the achievement; left for the viewer); *chief* top division of the shield; *lion passant guardant* lion standing, facing; *gules doubled argent*: red backed with silver.

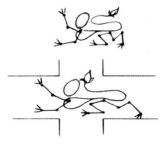

2 The lion has to be elongated in order to fit into the centre of the cross. Work from the bone structure and keep the drawing simple, ideally working from life —cats make good models, although traditionally heraldic animals are bold and fierce.

3 Once you have decided on your design, trace it out on to the paper or vellum in pencil outline, allowing a wide margin. The liveliness and strength of the drawing at this stage is critical. (You can trace from the finished piece which is shown at actual size on p107.)

Start with the lettering. This was done with ground Chinese stick ink and Mitchell nibs (motto with a No. 6 nib in simple capitals; the caption in a modernized gothic script, using a No. 4½ nib).

Add the gold next. Here, shell gold has been painted on and then polished with an agate burnisher (see pp98-9).

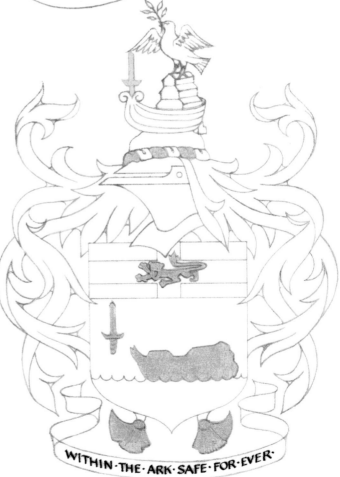

WITHIN·THE·ARK·SAFE·FOR·EVER·

The Armorial Bearings of
The Worshipful Company of Shipwrights

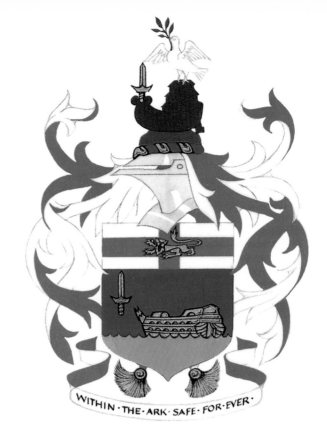

4 Now apply the broad areas of colour, using a sable brush. You can add one colour at a time, or work from top to bottom. Gouache (permanence A) is used for everything except the helmet, which is done in watercolour (indigo).

Colours must be bright, pure and bold. Gules —scarlet lake (plus permanent white and havannah lake for shading); argent —unpainted, with shadows of blue and grey; azure —ultramarine and cerulean (plus a little permanent white); vert —oxide of chromium (plus a little yellow ochre).

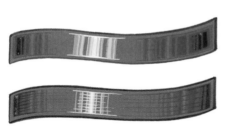

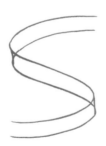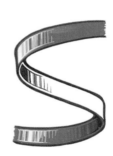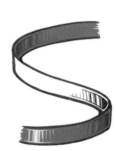

The Armorial Bearings of The Worshipful Company of Shipwrights

5 Mantling can be shaded to give a three-dimensional quality. Two methods are shown above: hatched gradated horizontal and vertical lines, and gradated vertical lines only. Remember that the light must appear to be falling from the top left.

Start by applying a layer of the base colour over the entire area. Mix a mid-light and a light tone by adding white to the base colour. Mix a mid-dark and a dark tone by adding havannah lake. Apply the tones to give a gradated effect, leaving a small strip of base colour between the tonal changes.

light		mid-dark
mid-light	base colour	dark

The dark outlines and white highlights (around the borders of the mantling) should be used very sparingly. Note that the curve of the folds can be reversed to alter the "fall" of the mantling.

6 Capturing the effect of light reflecting from metal takes practice, but it will become easier if you relate it to everyday objects, such as saucepans. Here darker tones have been built up by applying several layers of indigo watercolour, but you can try other colours, or gouache paints. As a final touch, add a faint tint of reflected colour from the mantling.

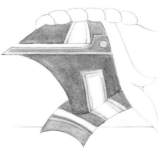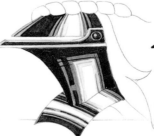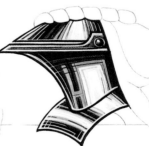

a First apply two washes of the lightest tones of indigo watercolour.

b Add a third layer of watercolour, in a slightly darker tone.

c Apply the darkest wash, the light and dark highlights, and a dark outline.

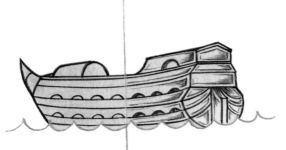

Burnished gold

Gold modelled with shading of sepia watercolour and yellow ochre gouache.

7 Subtle colouring of gold will enhance it and give a sculptural quality. This can be done at any stage after the gold is in place, but is perhaps best done before the outlining. Gold is tonally a brown colour, so use related colours for the modelling. Here the outline is in sepia watercolour, which is also used for some of the shading, together with yellow ochre gouache. Keep it simple.

8 The outlines will sharpen up the definition. Here they are painted in havannah lake.

The achievement is shown at actual size. If it is to be framed allow generous margins. In this case, the achievement was painted on vellum measuring 24 × 15cm (9½ × 6in). The second line of text sits 5cm (2in) from the edge of the bottom margin. Leave a gap between the paper and the glass of the frame.

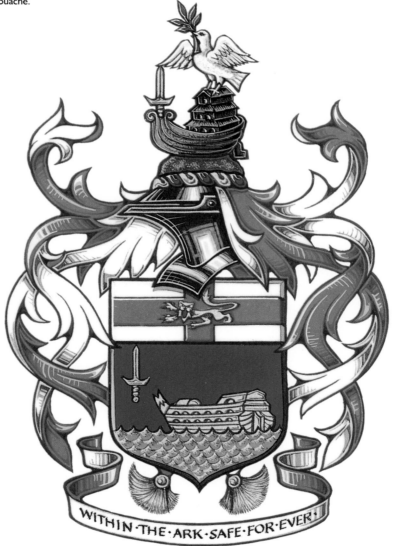

WITHIN·THE·ARK·SAFE·FOR·EVER

Heraldry by Irena Armstrong. By kind permission of The Worshipful Company of Shipwrights.

The Armorial Bearings of The Worshipful Company of Shipwrights

Garden Plan

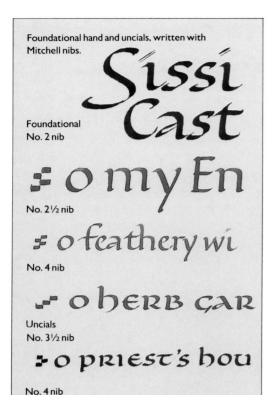

Foundational hand and uncials, written with Mitchell nibs.

Sissi Cast

Foundational
No. 2 nib

o my En

No. 2½ nib

o feathery wi

No. 4 nib

o herb car

Uncials
No. 3½ nib

o priest's hou

No. 4 nib

Squaring up
A plan, map or drawing can be enlarged on a grid. First draw a grid of squares on a tracing or copy of the plan. Extend a diagonal line to make an enlargement of the grid, of the same proportions, and with the same number of squares. The details from each original square can be transferred to the enlarged square.

THE design of a decorative map or plan depends on the successful combination of calligraphy and illustration. Begin by assembling reference material: the plan, the texts and the illustrations. You will have to be selective, as the inclusion of too many elements will look cluttered; the main aim should be to combine the various elements harmoniously. In this case, Sissinghurst Castle's literary associations made it easy to find suitable quotations.

You will need: basic equipment (*see pp36-7*), gouache (olive green, havannah lake, winsor green, lemon yellow, zinc white, yellow ochre), sable brush (No. 2), palette, coloured crayons, toothbrush, technical drawing pen, ruling pen, flexible curve, handmade paper (Chatham vellum).

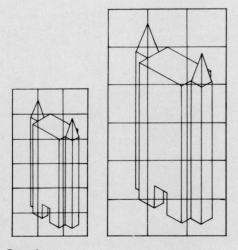

1 Make thumbnail layouts to decide on the format. You can square up and enlarge the plan on p111, or draw up your own plan.

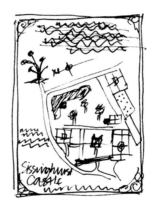

2 Having decided on the scripts, write out all the text. Here uncials are used for the labelling, and foundational hand for the quotations and the heading. Try alternative styles for the lettering and the illustrated features. Decide on a colour scheme (olive green and havannah lake are dominant in this plan) and work in colour from the beginning. Use layout paper, paper of a similar tone, or the same paper as for the finished piece.

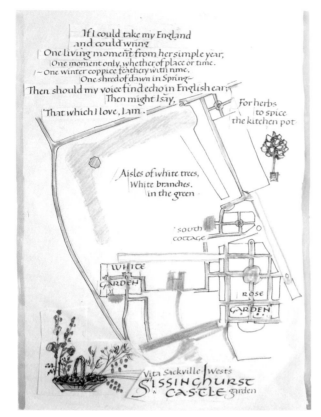

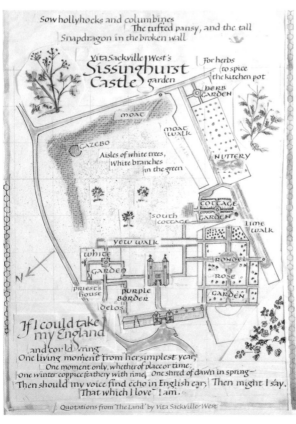

3 Start assembling the various parts, positioning the labels first and then the quotations. A layout offers an infinite number of possibilities which can be worked on by re-arranging the various elements on the plan. These two preliminary stages show how the large area of text and the heading were re-positioned to give a better balance. The border is used as a unifying element; the design is taken from the pattern of paving stones. The floral drawings are sketched with a felt pen, and broad areas of colour are blocked in with crayons.

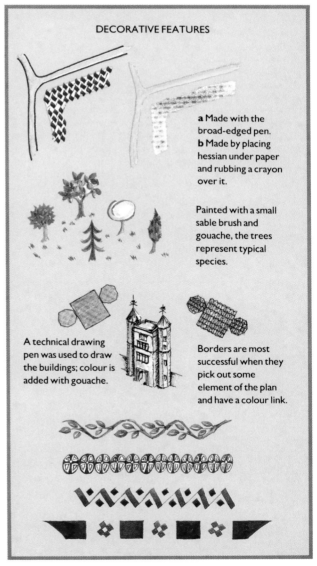

DECORATIVE FEATURES

a Made with the broad-edged pen.
b Made by placing hessian under paper and rubbing a crayon over it.

Painted with a small sable brush and gouache, the trees represent typical species.

A technical drawing pen was used to draw the buildings; colour is added with gouache.

Borders are most successful when they pick out some element of the plan and have a colour link.

GARDEN PLAN

4 Once you have decided on the arrangement, choose a paper, and trace down the outline of the plan. Plan your order of working. **a** The garden and house labels were written first in uncials. **b** The lines of the walks and road were drawn with a ruling pen, ruler, and a flexible curve. When dry, a thin wash of yellow ochre and olive green was added. **c** The texture of the moat, hedges and buildings was made with crayon and hessian. **d** Lines were ruled for the main text and the title, which were then written. **e** The background texture of the orchard was applied by spattering olive green gouache from a toothbrush (taking care to mask the rest of the plan first). When dry, the text was written in this area. **f** The outlines of the buildings were drawn with a technical drawing pen, and then a thin wash of gouache paint was added. **g** The lines of the border were drawn with a ruling pen and ink. **h** The roses and two herb plants were painted with thinned gouache, starting with the stems and gradually building up the detail (using olive and winsor green, havannah lake and white). **i** The final texts were placed to balance the design ("Sow hollyhocks ..." "For herbs..." and the credit line). **j** The border was painted.

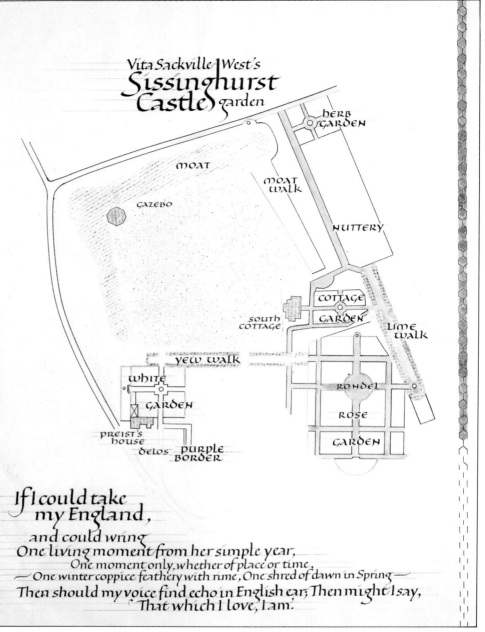

Vita Sackville West's
Sissinghurst Castle garden

HERB GARDEN

MOAT

MOAT WALK

GAZEBO

NUTTERY

COTTAGE GARDEN

SOUTH COTTAGE

LIME WALK

YEW WALK

WHITE GARDEN

RONDEL

ROSE GARDEN

PREIST'S HOUSE

DELOS

PURPLE BORDER

If I could take my England,
and could wring
One living moment from her simple year,
One moment only, whether of place or time,
— One winter coppice feathery with rime, One shred of dawn in Spring —
Then should my voice find echo in English ear; Then might I say,
That which I love, I am.

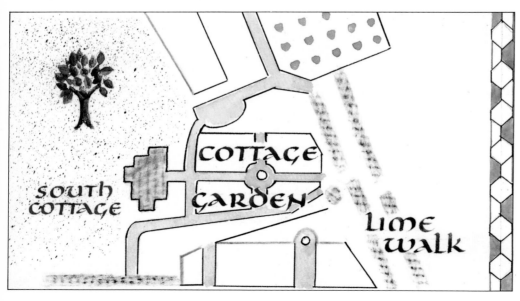

SOUTH COTTAGE

COTTAGE GARDEN

LIME WALK

Actual size (at borders) 44 × 29cm (17¼ × 11½in).
Garden plan by Christine Oxley.
From 'The Land' by Vita Sackville-West.
© First published by William Heinemann Ltd in 1926. Reprinted by permission of William Heinemann Ltd.

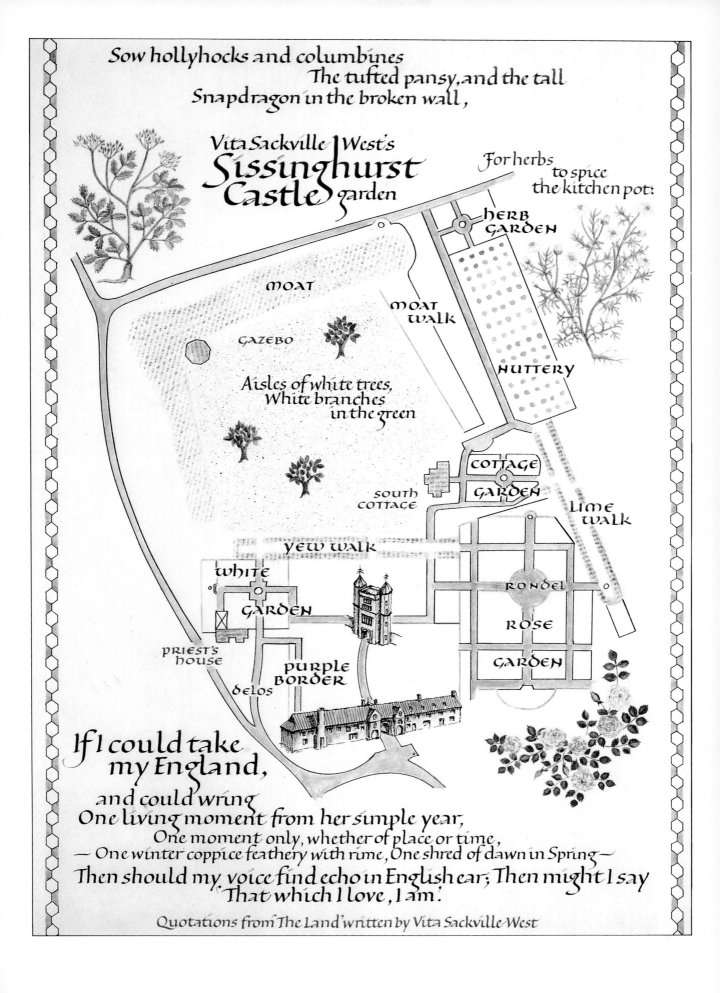

Sow hollyhocks and columbines
The tufted pansy, and the tall
Snapdragon in the broken wall,

Vita Sackville West's
Sissinghurst Castle garden

For herbs to spice the kitchen pot:

HERB GARDEN

MOAT

MOAT WALK

GAZEBO

Aisles of white trees,
White branches
in the green

NUTTERY

COTTAGE GARDEN

SOUTH COTTAGE

LIME WALK

YEW WALK

WHITE GARDEN

RONDEL

ROSE

GARDEN

PRIEST'S HOUSE

PURPLE BORDER

delos

If I could take
my England,
and could wring
One living moment from her simple year,
One moment only, whether of place or time,
— One winter coppice feathery with rime, One shred of dawn in Spring—
Then should my voice find echo in English ear; Then might I say
That which I love, I am!

Quotations from 'The Land' written by Vita Sackville West

Lettering on Ceramic

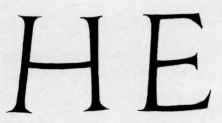

He

Versal letters must be distorted to adapt them for writing around a circle.

and
and
and

To add weight to these lower-case letters, simply widen the strokes in the same way as versals, imitating the weight of edged forms (see p50). Both the thickness of the letters and the serifs can be altered. Actual size (above), and reduced (below).

b c e f g
h i j k l m
n o p q r
s t u v w
x y z

Lettering with cold ceramic paint means that you can avoid using glazes and slips which have to be fired in a kiln. These paints do not give the professional finish of the traditional techniques, and, although they claim to be permanent, it is safer to use them for decoration only. Nevertheless they are fun to use, and are available in a range of bright colours.

Try different lettering styles – anything can be used (even your own handwriting) as long as it can be adapted for painting. You will need: basic equipment (see pp36-7), compasses, small brushes (sizes 0, 1 or 2, preferably sable, but synthetic hair is perfectly adequate), white spirit, soft rags, thin felt-tip pen, white ceramic plate (25.5cm/10in diameter for this project).

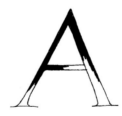

1 Try using the cold ceramic paint undiluted, and then thinned with a little white spirit. You will find it is very quick-drying. Clean brushes frequently with white spirit while working. Outline the letters first and then fill in the stems, aiming for an even cover. Make corrections by wiping off the wet paint with white spirit and a soft cloth. When finished, clean your brush in white spirit and wash it in soapy water. Allow the paint to dry for several hours.

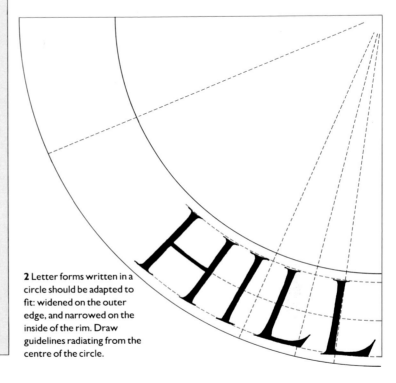

2 Letter forms written in a circle should be adapted to fit: widened on the outer edge, and narrowed on the inside of the rim. Draw guidelines radiating from the centre of the circle.

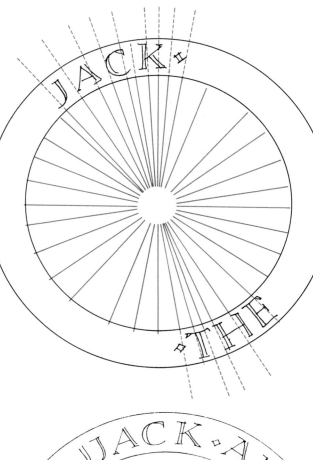

3 Draw the inner and outer edges of the rim with a pair of compasses. Use a ruler to draw straight lines across the diameter of the circle. This is essential for finished drawings, and can also be useful when planning roughs.

Capital letters are suitable for writing around a rim because of their geometric quality. Keep turning the drawing as you work so that you look directly at the letters. Letters which fill the entire rim are more effective.

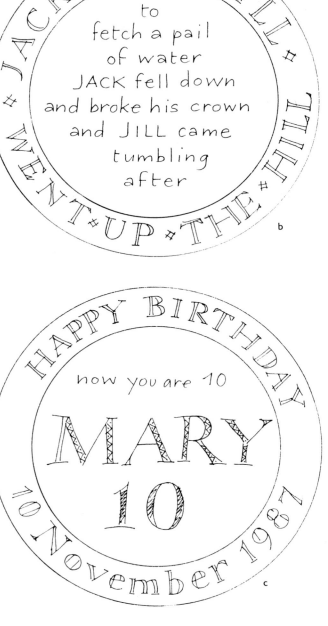

4 Make some rough drawings: **a** with the rim lettering running continuously around the plate; **b** with the writing broken at the centre to read from left to right. Making the text fit is a matter of trial and error until you have gained enough experience to judge spacing more accurately.

The central panel should fill the shape comfortably. **c** A decorated plate is an ideal gift for a birthday, or other commemorative occasion. Make the names the most dominant part of the design, and try a more decorative treatment for the letters, perhaps including an illustration.

113

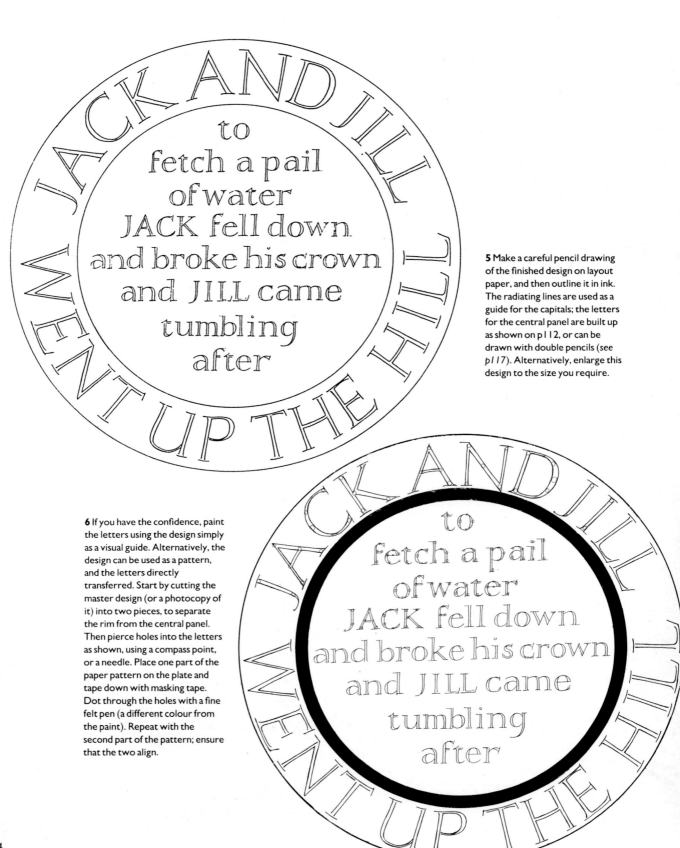

5 Make a careful pencil drawing of the finished design on layout paper, and then outline it in ink. The radiating lines are used as a guide for the capitals; the letters for the central panel are built up as shown on p112, or can be drawn with double pencils (*see p117*). Alternatively, enlarge this design to the size you require.

6 If you have the confidence, paint the letters using the design simply as a visual guide. Alternatively, the design can be used as a pattern, and the letters directly transferred. Start by cutting the master design (or a photocopy of it) into two pieces, to separate the rim from the central panel. Then pierce holes into the letters as shown, using a compass point, or a needle. Place one part of the paper pattern on the plate and tape down with masking tape. Dot through the holes with a fine felt pen (a different colour from the paint). Repeat with the second part of the pattern; ensure that the two align.

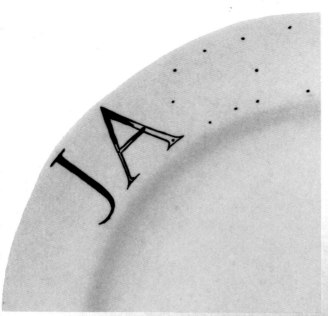

7 The outline of the letters can be drawn in with felt pen before painting, although as your confidence increases, you will be able to paint more freely with the brush, using only the dots as a guide. Decide on an order of working that suits you. If you intend painting the whole plate at one sitting, work out a logical sequence that allows for drying. It would perhaps be easiest in three stages: the top of the rim, the central panel, the bottom of the rim. When the paint has dried (to be safe allow a couple of days), wipe off any remaining felt pen with a damp cloth.

Actual size: diameter of plate 25.5cm (10in).
Lettering by Brenda Berman.

JACK AND JILL · WENT UP THE HILL ·

to
fetch a pail
of water
JACK fell down
and broke his crown
and JILL came
tumbling
after

115

Logo Design

A LOGO should be instantly identifiable in any situation – from a sign on the side of a van to a business card. The logo for "Helios" (which conveys a bold, confident image), is prepared to a very high finish for reproduction, using a method that can be adapted to a much larger scale and different materials.

The letters are based on a calligraphic form, and are drawn, rather than directly written with a broad-edged pen. Double pencils define the basic structure, and provide a starting point from which modifications can be made. You will need: basic equipment (*see pp36-7*), good quality line board, waterproof Indian ink, wax-free graphite paper, No. 1 pointed sable brush, fine mapping pen or technical drawing pen, white gouache and brush.

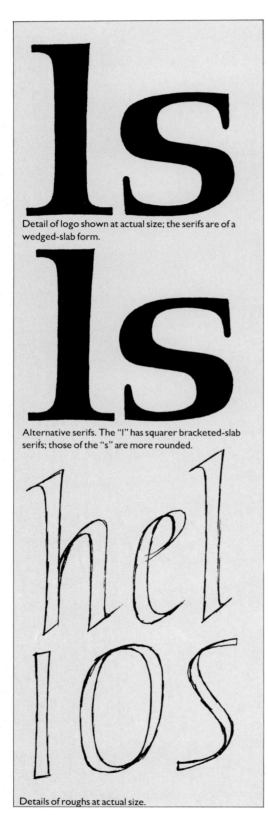

Detail of logo shown at actual size; the serifs are of a wedged-slab form.

Alternative serifs. The "I" has squarer bracketed-slab serifs; those of the "s" are more rounded.

Details of roughs at actual size.

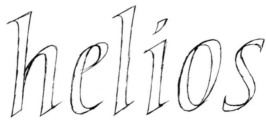

Capitals with swelled stems.

Italic lower-case letters; directly based on a calligraphic form.

Heavy-weight, wide capitals.

I With pencil or pen sketches explore a wide variety of letter forms, heights and weights. These roughs were drawn with a felt-tipped pen on layout paper. Imitating the forms made by a broad-edged pen takes a considerable amount of skill, so this stage can be done, roughly, with double pencils.

Helios

2 The rough selected for this logo uses a bold lower-case letter with an initial capital letter. The height of the lower-case letters is equivalent to approximately four nib-widths (or stem widths in this case), the capital is about five nib-widths high, and the ascender of the "l" just slightly higher.

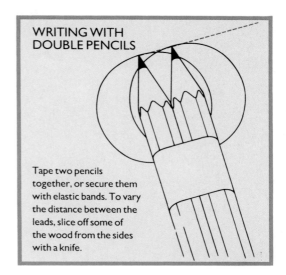

WRITING WITH DOUBLE PENCILS

Tape two pencils together, or secure them with elastic bands. To vary the distance between the leads, slice off some of the wood from the sides with a knife.

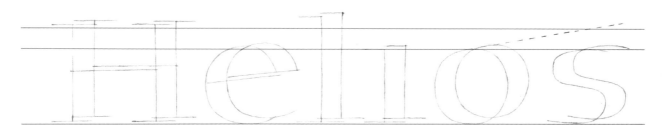

3 Rule up the writing lines on a sheet of layout paper and write out the basic form of the letters more accurately, using double pencils. Space the letters evenly along the line. For this design, the pencils are held at an angle of about 10° to the writing line (indicated by the red line).

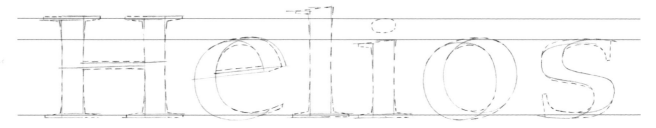

4 Place a second sheet of layout paper over the first, and trace through with an H pencil, making modifications to the letter forms. The adjustments made here are indicated by the dotted lines. The sides of the vertical stems were slightly curved, producing a narrower mid-point. The cross-over points of the curved letters were thickened to produce smooth, continuous inner and outer contours. The serifs are built up, with a wedged emphasis.

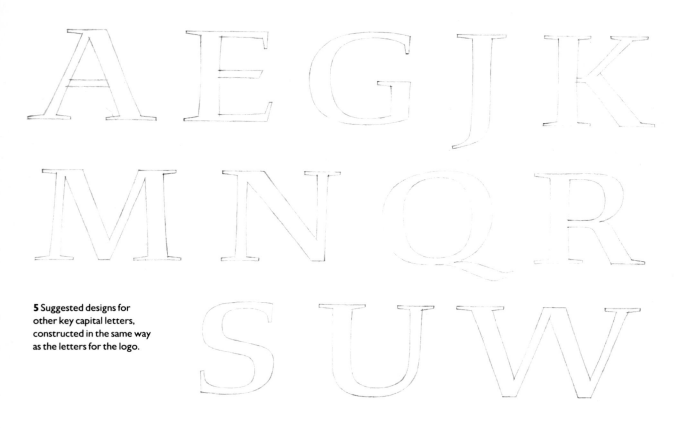

5 Suggested designs for other key capital letters, constructed in the same way as the letters for the logo.

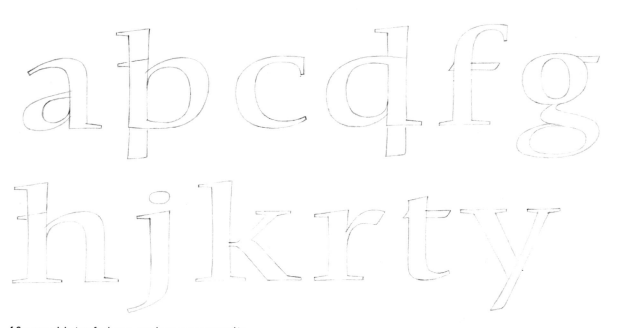

6 Suggested designs for lower-case letters constructed in the same way as the letters for the logo. The arched forms ("n" and "h"), and curved forms ("b" and "p", "q" and "d") can be drawn on the same basic form, reinforcing an awareness of the family likeness of letters within an alphabet.

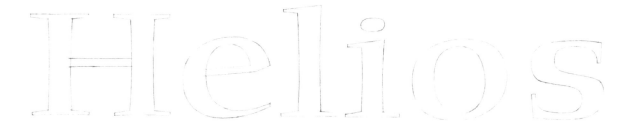

7 Make a further drawing on layout paper to finalize all the details. Then trace down on to the line board, using a sheet of rouge paper or graphite paper, and going over the drawing with a 2H pencil for an accurate outline.

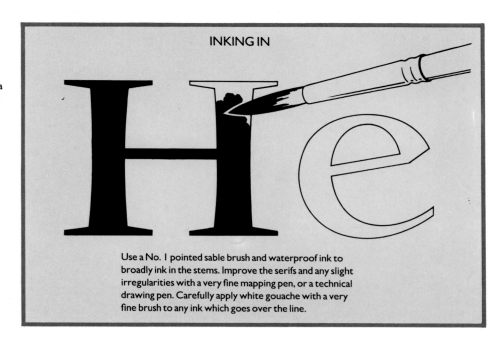

INKING IN

Use a No. 1 pointed sable brush and waterproof ink to broadly ink in the stems. Improve the serifs and any slight irregularities with a very fine mapping pen, or a technical drawing pen. Carefully apply white gouache with a very fine brush to any ink which goes over the line.

Helios

8 When all the inking in and tidying up is complete, erase the guidelines, and protect with an overlay. The artwork is now ready for use.

*Actual size of logo: 232 × 47mm
(9 × 1³/₄in)
Logo design by Tom Perkins.*

EMBOSSING

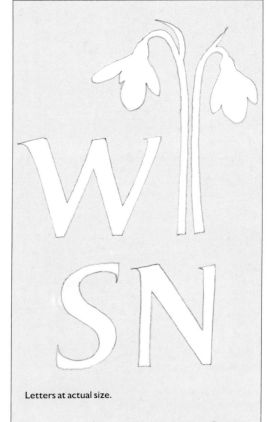

Letters at actual size.

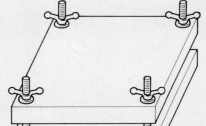

Hand press
The project is embossed by an ingenious method, but it does require a very light touch. If you find this difficult, try using a small hand press (basically two flat pieces of wood fastened by four butterfly nuts). The paper can be dampened before it is put in the press with the lino. Place a piece of foam rubber 25mm (1 in) thick, or an expanded polystyrene tile, between the paper and the press. This will impress the design into the paper. The lino should not be larger than the press.

THE PLAY of light and shadow on embossed lettering has a pleasing, subtle quality. The embossing method shown here requires a very light touch, but will produce excellent results. It also allows for embossing on to both dry and damp paper. If you want to combine embossing with pen-written letters, emboss with dry paper; a damp paper will give a better impression but it will be difficult to write on. (To dampen, immerse paper for a few seconds, remove, and absorb excess water with blotting paper or clean towels.) You will need: basic equipment (*see pp36-7*), piece of lino (at least 11.5 × 27cm/4½ × 10½in), lino-cutting tools (Mitchell Nos. 1, 5, 6), graphite carbon paper, paper (dampened Rives printmaking paper was used), dogtooth agate burnisher, and stiff brush.

I Draw the design on to layout paper. (Trace from the letters in the box, or make an enlarged photocopy of the above). Accurate drawing now will ensure an accurate cutting guide. Very thin strokes will be difficult to cut. Reverse the design on to another sheet by one of the following methods:

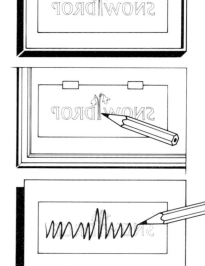

Place the design face down on a light box (a box with a perspex or glass top, lit from below with electric light). Trace the reversed outline on the back, or tape a second sheet of layout paper on top and trace off.

Tape the design on a window pane and trace over the back of the outline, or tape a second sheet of layout paper over it, and trace on to it, outlining the lettering in reverse.

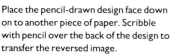

Place the pencil-drawn design face down on to another piece of paper. Scribble with pencil over the back of the design to transfer the reversed image.

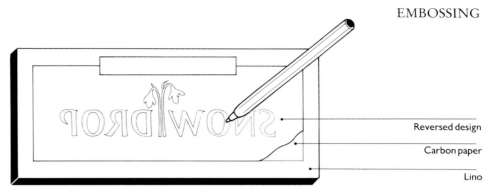

2 Transfer the reversed drawing on to the lino using carbon paper. Tape the design down, and go over the outline with a hard pencil or biro for a crisp line. The size of the lino is not critical if you are using a burnisher.

Reversed design

Carbon paper

Lino

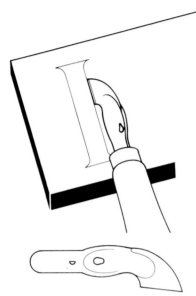

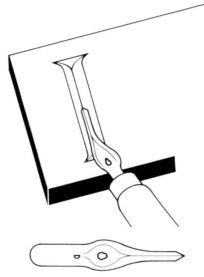

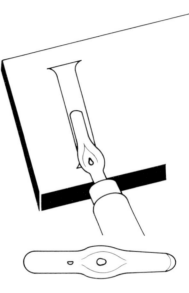

3 Lino is easier to cut if it is warmed. First cut the outlines of the letters, using a No. 5 cutter (a flat blade). Hold it at an angle to prevent undercutting, which would weaken the edges. This first cut should prevent chipped edges.

4 Use a No. 1 cutter (a small v-profile) to begin cutting into the letters, moving from the corners of the letters and the serifs, and then up the centre of the strokes. Make sure that you always push the cutter away from yourself.

5 Use a round cutter (No. 6) to scoop out the remaining lino. Take care near the edges, and aim for a smooth, clean, even, and rounded cut. Any irregularity will show up. Go over the fine lines and corners with the No. 1 cutter.

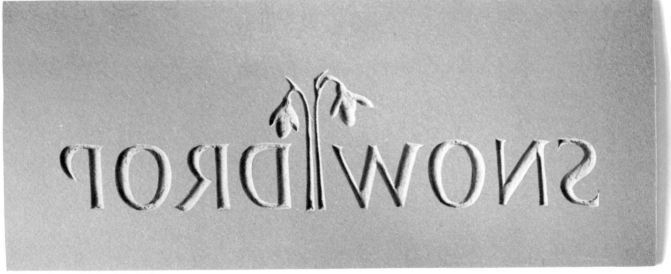

6 When all the cutting has been done, brush out the letter with a stiff brush (or an old toothbrush) and then wipe with a cloth, to remove all fragments of lino. Recheck the smoothness of the cutting.

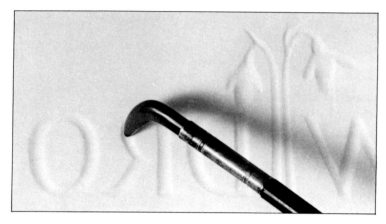

7 Embossing can be done on dry paper, but dampened paper will give a better impression. Place the lino on a flat surface and lay the paper on the lino. Hold the paper down firmly with one hand, or carefully weight it down at the edge with something heavy (and clean). Rub carefully but firmly with clean fingers over the letters to make a slight impression as a guide for burnishing. Use the burnisher with a very light touch. First rub along the stems of the letters, with the flat of the burnisher, then with the heel go carefully around the edges of the letters, and finally go down into the grooves. (Note: the embossing is indented, although it appears raised.)

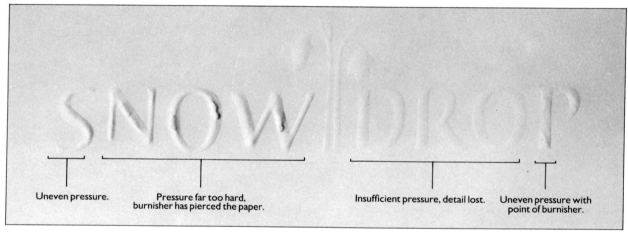

Uneven pressure.   Pressure far too hard, burnisher has pierced the paper.   Insufficient pressure, detail lost.   Uneven pressure with point of burnisher.

8 Rub with slow, firm, even pressure so that all the letters are embossed to an equal level, using the heel of the burnisher. Remove the paper carefully. If there are faults, it is almost impossible to replace the paper and it is better to make another impression.

Actual size (without margins): 6 × 22cm (2 ¼ × 8 ⅝ in). Embossing by Susan Hufton.

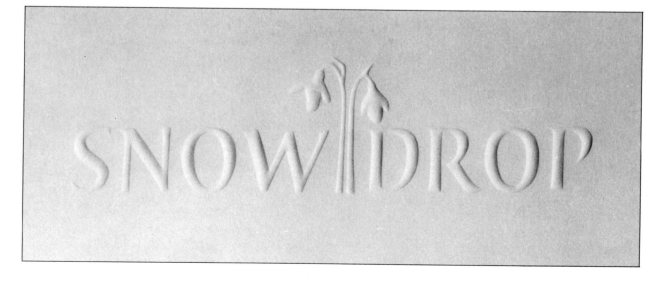

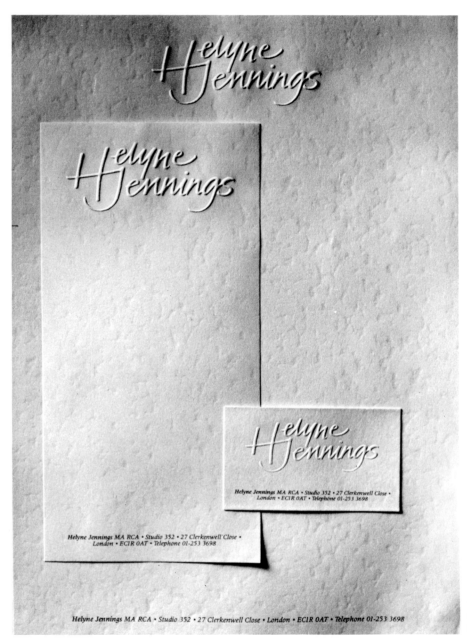

Embossing can be done commercially by a printer. The letters for the name on this letterheading were freely written with a pointed brush and ink. The printer used the artwork to make a plate from which the print was made. (The address is typeset and printed red, on cream paper.) Stationery by Lilly Lee.

This embossing was done from letters cut from card. The design for the letters was originally made at about 42 × 30cm (16½ × 12in) with automatic pens. The letters were cut out of card. It was embossed on to dampened thick cartridge paper with a roller press.
Embossed letters by Nick Stewart.

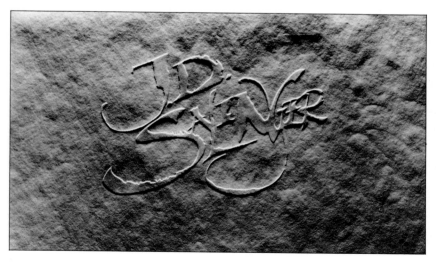

RUBBER STAMPS

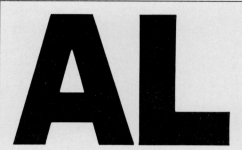

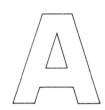

These simple block letters are based on a sans serif typeface. All non-symmetrical letters and designs *must* be reversed (*see p120*) before the stamps are cut. This is not necessary for symmetrical forms such as this "A".

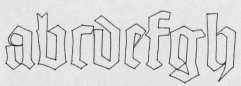

A typeface with heavy slab serifs – a good bold shape for a rubber stamp.

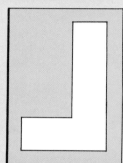

The first printed type in the mid-15th century used gothic calligraphic forms.

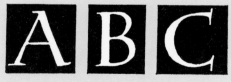

Versal letters can be used for monograms and letter headings. To retain the hairline serifs, cut out the letter, rather than cutting out the surrounding area.

Start off with simple letters and decorative motifs. When looking for suitable letter forms, choose bold shapes and avoid fine serifs and hairlines. Typefaces can also be used as a source of inspiration.

THIS simple printing technique requires few materials and only a little practice to achieve fun, decorative results. You can use rubber stamp letters as monograms to liven up letter headings and envelopes, or to create abstract patterns for decorative borders on greetings cards, and even wrapping paper.

Start with a very simple design. Remember that you must always cut non-symmetrical designs in reverse, and that what you cut away will not print. You will need: basic equipment (*see pp36-7*), plastic eraser, needle (or compasses), lino-cutting tool (v-profile) and holder, scalpel, and stamp pad.

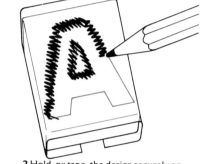

1 First design or trace your letter. Start with a simple shape so that you can concentrate on the method.

2 Hold, or tape, the design securely on the eraser (reversed if necessary), and trace with a pencil.

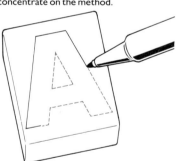

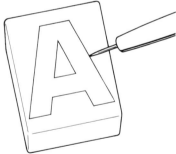

3 Define the outline more clearly, using a fine felt pen to retain a clear image while cutting. Do not use a ball-point pen.

4 Score the outline lightly with a needle. Angle the point away from the letter to prevent undercutting.

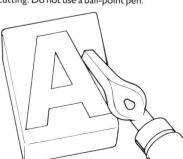

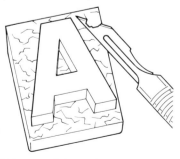

5 Cut carefully around the outline with a small v-profile lino-cutting tool, held at a shallow angle.

6 Cut away all the surplus with a scalpel. Take trial prints and make final adjustments

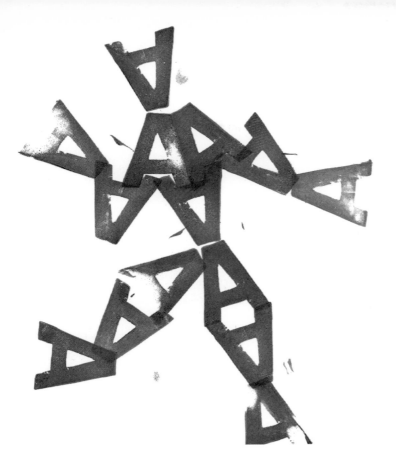

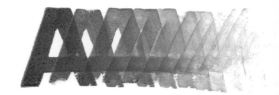

When printing, press on to the inked stamp pad and then press down firmly on to the paper, without wobbling. Re-ink between stampings, or the tone of the print will fade. Clean the ink off the stamp with a damp sponge when you have finished, or when you change colours.

To make opposite shapes, cut one design, stamp it on to a second eraser, and then cut out the reverse areas. Small dots can be made by twisting the very tip of a scraperboard tool. Use ink pads of different colours, or buy an empty stamp pad and mix your own inks.

All-over patterns (made by repeatedly stamping a design) are easy to align if the design goes right to the edge of the stamp. To align a line of letters accurately, make sure that they are all of the same height and that they sit on the same baseline. Mark the top of the letter on the back of the stamp.

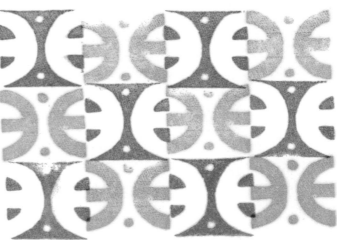

Rubber stamps by Patricia Gidney.

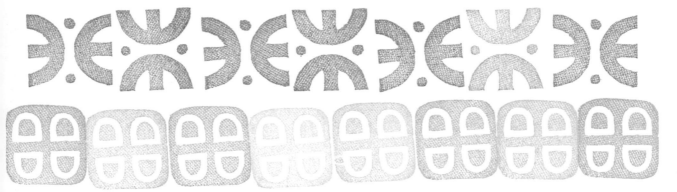

Letter Rubbings

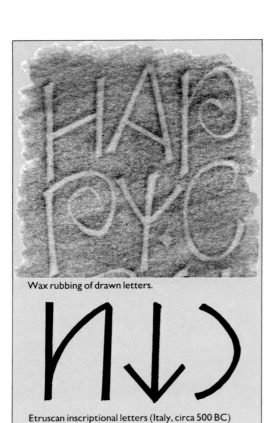

Wax rubbing of drawn letters.

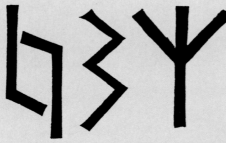

Etruscan inscriptional letters (Italy, circa 500 BC) have strong vertical forms.

Runes are ancient Germanic letters, which were believed to have a magical symbolism. (Designs by Rudolf Koch)

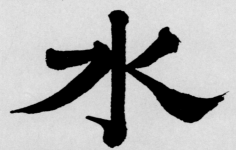

Painted Chinese character. Rubbing gives the appearance of raised embroidery.

THIS very effective technique simply involves cutting letters out of card and making rubbings of them with crayons. It is easy to do and seems to actually improve the appearance of letter forms; it also gives the impression that the rubbings have been made from more sustantial carved letters. Have a look at ancient forms, such as runes, or other writing systems, such as Chinese or Arabic and use the forms in a more abstract way.

This Christmas card combines letter forms based on various ancient forms with those of a more contemporary influence to give a decorative pattern. Rubbings can be made with coloured crayon, pencil, pastel, wax crayons; a wash of paint or ink over the rubbing will give an interesting effect. You will need: basic equipment (*see pp36-7*); wax crayon.

Incised rubbings Cut the letter or shape out of card. Lay a piece of paper over the cut-out and rub with a crayon. Rubbed letters tend to be wider than the originals. Stick the card to a base if the letters have enclosed spaces (such as "A").

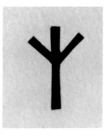
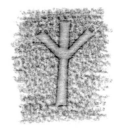

Raised rubbings Glue the cut-out shape or letter on to a piece of card. Make a rubbing with crayon. Rubbed letters look narrower than the originals. Try varying the direction of the strokes, or rubbing from one direction only.

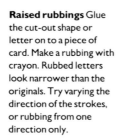
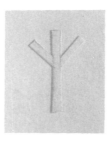
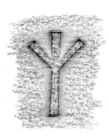

Experiments Different combinations will give varying effects: repeated rubbings produce a textural, abstract pattern; combining incised and raised rubbings varies the shading; different papers affect the definition; rubbing with a burnisher, rather than a crayon, will give a shallow blind embossing.

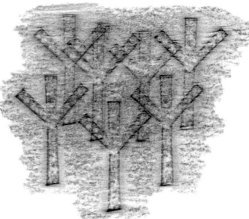

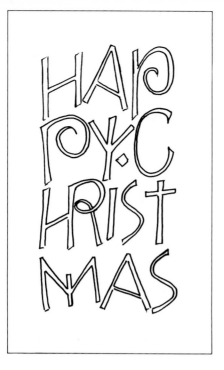

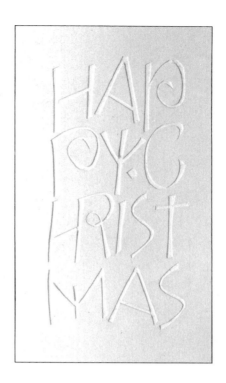

Trace the design on to thick cartridge paper and glue it to a piece of board with rubber cement. Cut out the letters with a scalpel, refining their forms as you cut. Cutting towards you will help to produce smooth lines. Make sure that the counters of the letters remain glued in place.

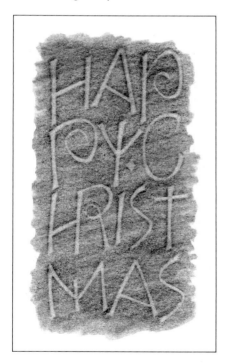

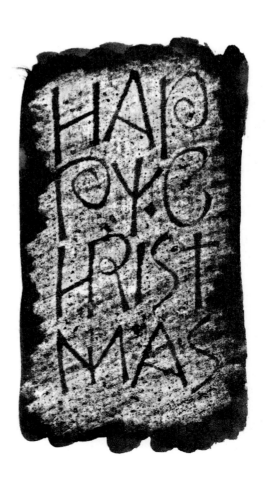

The wax crayon rubbing (above) was made on Chinese paper. The edges of the paper have been torn after being "painted" with a line of clear water. The paper was then glued on to a folded card. (Right) this rubbing was done with a white wax candle, and then black ink was brushed over it.

Actual size: 12 × 6cm (4³⁄₄ × 2¹⁄₂in).
Letter rubbing by Susanne Haines.

Experimental Lettering

WHEN you have the confidence, try becoming a little inventive and exploring a more experimental approach to your lettering. In this project, the capital letters are developed in a personal way that breaks the rules which can be so hard to learn at the beginning. The project starts by looking at an historical example, but soon departs from it – the number of pen strokes used to make the letters is increased to give some double strokes, and the pen is turned to very different angles; then the letter weight and the line space are altered. All of these changes have a dramatic effect on the tonal contrast and textural variety of a piece of writing. You will need: basic equipment (*see pp36-7*).

Mitchell round hand nibs

No. 1 nib

No. 2 nib

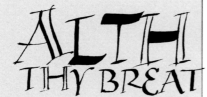

No. 4 nib

A modernized interpretation of Roman square capital letters (from the 4th or 5th century). The basically flat pen angle is not constant – it is frequently twisted while forming the strokes.

1 Start by selecting a basic script. The historical example on which these letters are based involves some complex handling of the pen, and lends itself well to experimentation. First write out the letters, making them as close to the original as possible; then try some variations. This selection of letters shows some of the variety that can be achieved by turning the pen to very different angles for some or all of the strokes in a letter.

BLOW BLOW
THOU WINTER WIND
THOU ART NOT
SO UNKIND
AS MAN'S
INGRATITUDE:
THY TOOTH
IS NOT SO KEEN
BECAUSE THOU
ART NOT SEEN
ALTHOUGH
THY BREATH
BE RUDE.

a

2 Begin by writing out the text as a block of capitals **a**, using the basic letter forms, written with a wide pen (No. 1). Close word spacing and virtually no line space will emphasize the textural pattern. Use only a baseline.

For the next pieces, try writing without lines. **b** Keeping the same letter height, introduce some letter variations and see how the tone and weight changes. **c** Now use two thinner nibs as well, and change the letter height and weight more frequently.

BLOW, BLOW,
THOU WINTER WIND
THOU ART NOT
SO UNKIND
AS MAN'S
INGRATITUDE:
THY TOOTH IS NOT SO KEEN
BECAUSE THOU ART NOT SEEN,
ALTHOUGH
d THY BREATH BE RUDE.

BLOW, BLOW,
THOU WINTER WIND
THOU ART NOT
SO UNKIND
AS MAN'S
INGRATITUDE:
THY TOOTH
IS NOT SO KEEN
BECAUSE THOU
ART NOT SEEN,
ALTHOUTH
THY BREATH
BE RUDE.
b

d Keeping a similar emphasis for most of the words, increase the space between some of the lines, and alter the line breaks.

*Actual size of **d** (text area): 175 × 105mm (7 × 4in)*
Calligraphy by Lilly Lee.

BLOW, BLOW,
THOU WINTER WIND
THOU ART NOT SO UNKIND
AS MAN'S INGRATITUDE:
THY TOOTH IS NOT SO KEEN
BECAUSE THOU ART
NOT SEEN,
ALTHOUGH
c THY BREATH BE RUDE.

129

HERE is an opportunity to really let go, to experience the sheer enjoyment of the pen, playing with the pattern and impact of the letters and the words, and experimenting with materials; for while it is wise to "look before you leap", do not let concern for achieving perfection in your letter forms inhibit you from a more spontaneous approach, or from exploring the possibilities of alternative techniques and combining unlikely materials.

Make use of a wide variety of traditional materials, and try improvising with others. Choose some wording – song titles, popular expressions, dictionary definitions, proverbs – and use your imagination.

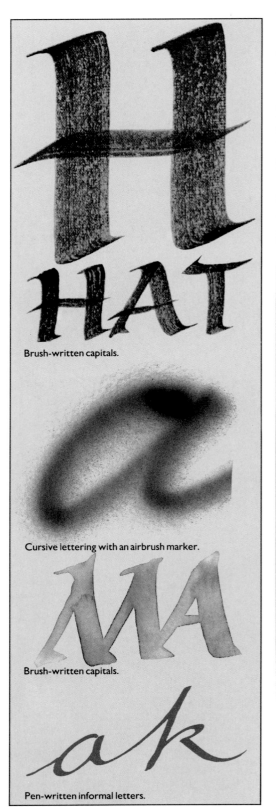

Brush-written capitals.

Cursive lettering with an airbrush marker.

Brush-written capitals.

Pen-written informal letters.

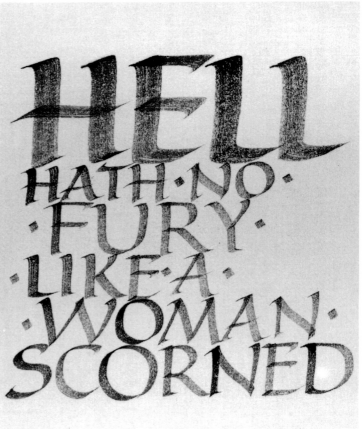

I Chisel-edged synthetic brushes and black gouache on cotton fabric. Prepare (or size) the fabric by soaking it in water with some PVA, letting it dry and then ironing it. The brush was held at a constant angle for most strokes.

130

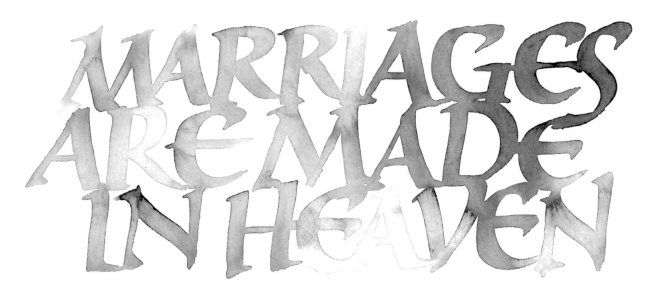

2 Chisel-edged brush on watercolour paper, written with clean water. While still wet, ink was spotted on at random, so that it spread through the strokes. The brush has been twisted to various angles, giving a wedged appearance to some of the strokes.

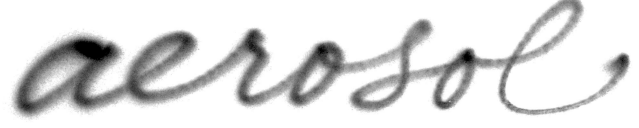

3 An airbrush marker is ideally suited to this cursive letter form, which is written with a continuous line.

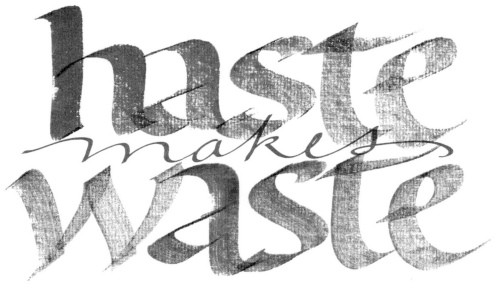

4 A flat, thin piece of balsa wood, dipped in ink and written on watercolour paper produces this textured appearance.

131

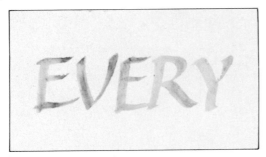

a Write the letters with masking fluid and allow to dry.

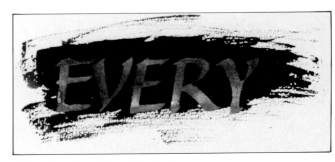

b Brush on paint or ink and allow to dry.

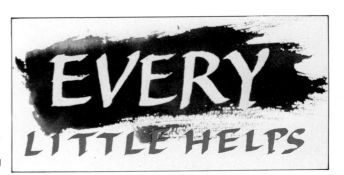

5 Resist is a technique involving two materials which do not mix, thus allowing you to protect areas of a surface while you apply another substance. When removed, the resists reveal the surface beneath. Several layers can be built up in this way, which is particularly effective with translucent colour.

Masking fluid is a popular, easy method. It can be used in pens, but it will ruin brushes. Clean the pen frequently, as masking fluid solidifies quickly. It can be diluted with water for a better flow. When dry, rub it off the paper with an eraser.

c Rub off the masking fluid and write the remaining text.

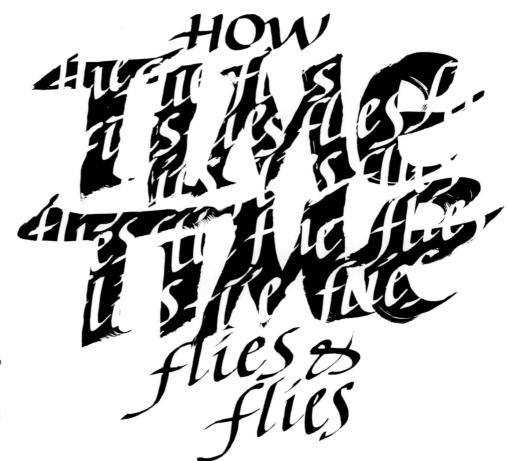

6 The word "how" was written first with a metal nib in ink. Then "flies" was written in masking fluid with a metal nib. When dry, "time" was written twice with a brush. The masking fluid was removed when the ink dried, and "flies" was written in pen and ink.

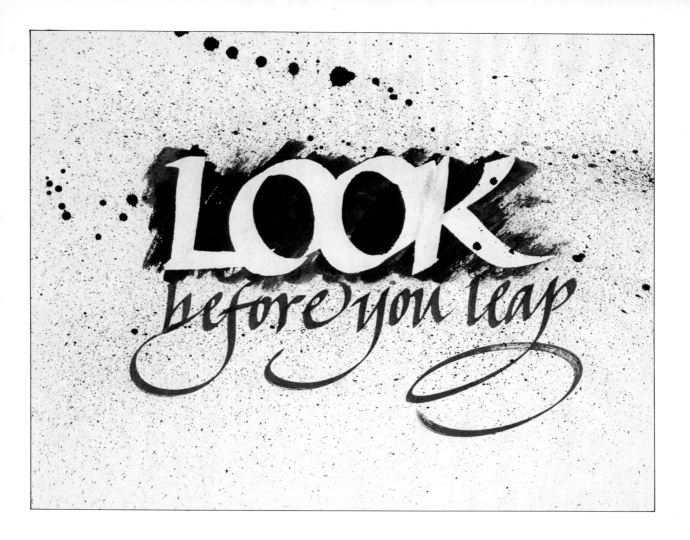

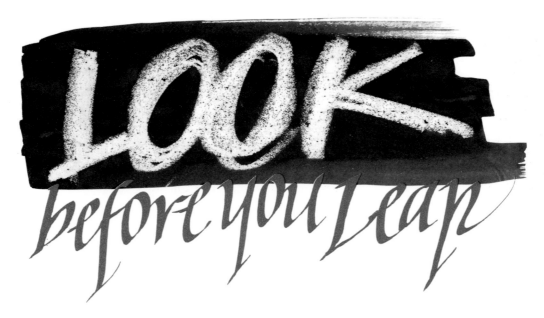

7 (Top) "Look" was written with masking fluid and balsa wood. When dry, mask the surrounding area with newspaper, dip a toothbrush in paint and draw the end of a pencil across the bristles. The drier the paint, the smaller the spatter dots. The small writing was then made with a felt pen. (Bottom) "Look" was written loosely with a wax crayon and then ink was brushed over. Finally, the smaller letters were written with red paint.

133

Lightning

NEVER
Strikes
the Same
PLACE
Twice

8 Bleach, an unlikely writing medium, produces surprisingly exciting effects, particularly when used on top of fountain pen ink. At the borders of the strokes all the various dyes in the ink are separated out, giving purple and brown hues; the centres of the strokes become glowing highlights, where the ink has been totally bleached away. However, use bleach with caution as it is poisonous. Always wash writing tools after use and do not use good brushes. (Above) Diluted fountain pen ink was brushed over heavy watercolour paper, and while still fairly wet, the word "lightning" was rapidly written. (Right) A wash of diluted fountain pen ink was applied with a broad brush and allowed to dry, before the writing was done with a piece of balsa wood dipped in bleach, using rapid, angular strokes.

Calligraphy by Lilly Lee

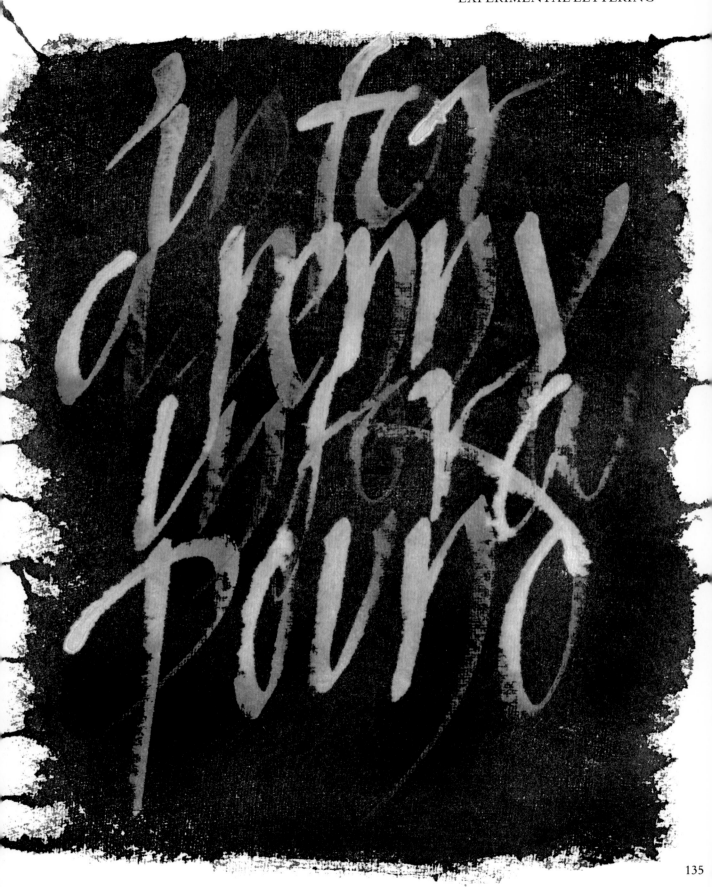

THE CALLIGRAPHERS

The calligraphers whose work is featured in the "gallery" section of the book are indexed on these pages. Biographies are given of those calligraphers who have contributed work to the other sections of the book.

IRENA ARMSTRONG
Irena joined a calligraphy evening class as a distraction from pressure of work running a London charity. Within a year she began a full-time course at Reigate School of Art and Design, where she gained a Diploma in Calligraphy, Illumination and Heraldry in 1984. She now works freelance.
HERALDRY, p104

BRENDA BERMAN
Originally studied painting at Bath Academy of Art, and taught for several years. Became interested in lettering while administering a small commercial printing works, and then studied for the Lettering Diploma at the City and Guilds of London Art School. Has subsequently returned there as course organizer and specialist calligrapher. Carries out freelance work on many aspects of lettering and letter design.
LETTERING ON CERAMIC p112

LINDSAY CASTELL
Graduate of Bristol University. She holds the Diploma in Calligraphy and Bookbinding from the Roehampton Institute (Digby Stuart College) and has worked as an assistant to Donald Jackson. She now works as a freelance calligrapher. Her work has been exhibited in both the UK and the USA.
FOUNDATIONAL HAND p50
CAPITALS p52

GERALD FLEUSS
Studied calligraphy with Ann Camp at Digby Stuart College. He now works as a freelance calligrapher and illuminator and has carried out many commissions for both private individuals and corporate bodies. He also has work in public collections both at home and in the USA. He is a Fellow of the Society of Scribes and Illuminators, and a Member of the Art Workers Guild. Visiting lecturer at Digby Stuart College.
WINE LABEL p81
ILLUMINATED PANEL p100

PATRICIA GIDNEY
Trained in shop and store display at Medway College of Design, and worked as a window display artist until going to Digby Stuart College to study calligraphy with Ann Camp for three years, obtaining the diploma in 1984. She now works as a freelance calligrapher, and teaches at workshops and residential courses.
GOTHIC p58
QUOTATION p70
CHRISTMAS CARD p74
RUBBER STAMPS p124

GAYNOR GOFFE
After several years teaching geography in secondary school, Gaynor trained in Calligraphy, Heraldry and Illumination at Reigate School of Art and Design (1975-8). Elected Fellow of the Society of Scribes and Illuminators in 1978. She worked as an assistant to Donald Jackson; she is now a freelance calligrapher and part-time teacher of calligraphy at Digby Stuart College, and on various short courses. Her work has appeared in several recent publications.
PRINTED STATIONERY p84
CALENDAR p88

SUSAN HUFTON
Susan first studied calligraphy as part of a B.Ed. degree. After teaching for three years, she decided to carry her studies further, and she now holds the Diploma in Advanced Calligraphy and Bookbinding from Digby Stuart College. She has taught at evening classes and workshops. In 1986 she was awarded a Crafts Council advanced

training grant to study lettercutting with Tom Perkins.
UNCIALS p54
VERSALS p56
EMBOSSING p120

LILLY LEE
Two short residential courses with Ann Hechle confirmed a consuming interest in calligraphy. From 1979-82 she studied at Digby Stuart College, and was then awarded a Crafts Council grant which enabled her to study with Richard Kindersley, Donald Jackson and Sheila Waters. She has now set up her own workshop in London, and works as a freelance calligrapher, specializing in commercial work (packaging, book jackets etc). She also works as a part-time tutor. Her work has been widely exhibited, and included in many publications.
MANUSCRIPT BOOK p92
EXPERIMENTAL LETTERING p128.

CHRISTINE OXLEY
Studied at Reigate School of Art and Design from 1974-9 where she gained the Diploma in Heraldry, Calligraphy and Illumination. Since leaving art school she has taught calligraphy at evening classes, and at residential courses throughout Britain. She works as a freelance calligrapher, producing work to commission and for exhibition.
GARDEN PLAN p108

ANDREW PARKINSON
Became interested in calligraphy while he was still at school. He studied design and art history in Surrey, and read history at Cambridge University. He now runs a calligraphy and graphic design business near London. His particular interests are quill cutting, copperplate and historical design. He is author of the recently published *Pens and Calligraphy* (Rexel).
COPPERPLATE p62
INVITATION p80

TOM PERKINS
Studied calligraphy at Reigate School of Art and Design and later lettercarving in stone with Richard Kindersley. He has undertaken many commissions since 1978 and participated in exhibitions both in the UK and abroad. His work is featured in several recent publications on lettering and calligraphy, and is in both private and public collections. Since 1983 he has been a visiting lecturer in calligraphy and lettering at the Roehampton Institute (Digby Stuart College).
LOGO DESIGN p116

GLOSSARY

ARCH a curved letter stroke which emerges from, or joins on to a stem.

ARM horizontal or diagonal limb of a letter.

ARTWORK finished work prepared for reproduction.

ASCENDER stroke which extends above the x-height of lower-case letters.

BASELINE or writing line, on which the base of the x-height of letters sits.

BODY-HEIGHT see x-height.

BOOKHAND writing style used to write texts of manuscript books.

BOWL curved letter strokes which enclose a counter.

BURNISH polish to a shine. Usually of gold, using a burnishing tool made from agate, or with a piece of silk.

CAPITAL also referred to as majuscule and upper case.

CENTRE to align text so that it is symmetrically, or visually balanced on a vertical line.

COMPLEMENTARY COLOUR the colour which contrasts with another most strongly (e.g. red and green, yellow and violet, blue and orange).

CONTE CRAYON crayon made from graphite and coloured clay.

COUNTER enclosed space within a letter.

CROSSBAR horizontal letter stroke.

CURSIVE informal, flowing style of writing.

DECKLE EDGE rough natural edge on handmade paper

DESCENDER stroke which descends below the x-height of lower-case letters.

DRAGON'S BLOOD rouge paper, used for tracing.

DUMMY mock-up for a manuscript book.

EMBOSS to impress paper surface into low relief.

EXEMPLAR an alphabet model, for copying.

FLEXIBLE CURVE a plastic-covered metal rod which you can bend to the required curve and use as a template.

FLOURISH a decorative extension of a pen stroke.

FORMAT overall shape of a piece of work.

FRENCH CURVE plastic template with a variety of curves.

GESSO fine plaster and adhesive, used as a base for raised gilding.

GILDING to apply gold.

GOUACHE water-based opaque paint. Also known as designer's colour, or body colour.

GUM ARABIC gum used as an addition to water-based paint to increase its fluidity, and to prevent it from rubbing off.

GUM AMMONIAC resin used in liquid form as a base for gilding.

GUM SANDARAC resin, which, when finely ground and dusted lightly on to paper before writing, will prevent the ink from spreading along the fibres. Particularly useful when writing names on certificates etc, which have been printed on a paper that is not suited to handwriting.

HAND writing style, or script

HAIRLINE finest line made by the pen.

ILLUMINATION decoration with colour and gold.

LINE SPACE space between baselines.

LOGO or logotype. A trademark or emblem, using letters, a word, or a symbol.

LOWER CASE typographic term for minuscule or small letter.

MAJUSCULE capital letter.

MANUSCRIPT a handwritten book.

MASKING TAPE a light-tack adhesive tape.

MEDIUM the binder in which pigment, or colour is held, and thus the kind of paint.

MINUSCULE small, or lower-case letter.

PALIMPSEST a re-used manuscript, generally on vellum, where the original text has been erased to make room for the next.

PASTE-UP an arrangement of a design, cut up and pasted on to a sheet of paper or board.

PMT photo mechanical transfer (see pp 66-7).

PVA polyvinyl acetate. Used as an adhesive for paper; also as a base for a simple method of gilding.

QUILL pen made from the flight feather of a goose, turkey or swan. The method for cutting a quill is similar to that shown for the reed or bamboo (p39), although quills must first be hardened and prepared.

RESIST technique involving two materials which do not mix.

SANS SERIF letter form without serifs, used of type.

SCRAPERBOARD board coated with a chalky surface. Ink is brushed over it, and an image is scraped through to the white layer below, with a pointed tool, to give a crisp line.

SCREENPRINT method of printing. The design is transferred on to a screen mesh (either photographically, or cut from an adhesive layer of paper, rather like a stencil). The ink is drawn across the screen and is forced through the unfilled areas on to the paper below.

SCRIPT writing style. Also sometimes used to imply a cursive style, or a copperplate typeface.

SERIF the fine strokes which terminate the main strokes of a letter form: for instance, pen-written letters can be made with hooked, wedged, hairline, club or slab serifs, or without serifs; drawn letters and type have even more variety.

SIZE adhesive sealant.

SKELETON LETTER letter reduced to its essential form, drawn with a single, unweighted line.

SPREAD double-page opening of a book.

STEM vertical stroke of a letter.

TRIM MARKS marks drawn at the corners of a piece of work prepared for printing, to indicate where the paper should be cut.

TYPEFACE the design of type; also its printed impression.

UPPER CASE typographic term for capital letters.

VELLUM calfskin prepared as a writing surface. Also used to describe paper which attempts to imitate it.

WATERCOLOUR translucent water-based colours.

WEIGHT of a letter, the relation of the nib-width used to the x-height of the letter.

X-HEIGHT the height of the main part (or body) of a letter, without ascenders and descenders. Typographic term.

INDEX

V

Van Stone, Mark, 16
vellum, 42
versals, 56-7

W

watercolours, 40, 41
waterproof ink, 40
Waters, Sheila, 30
weight:
    letterforms, 45, 48
    paper, 43
wine labels, 81-3
working order, 65
working position, 46
wove paper, 42

Z

Z-fold, 76

ACKNOWLEDGEMENTS

THE AUTHOR and The Paul Press Ltd would like to thank Falkiner Fine Papers, Philip Poole, Daler Rowneys, and the Universal Penman for their advice and help in lending materials.

The Paul Press would also like to thank the following organizations to whom copyright in the photographs noted belongs:
50 (Harley MS 2904) reproduced by courtesy of the Trustees of the British Museum; 52 by courtesy of the Board of Trustees of the Victoria and Albert Museum; 54 reproduced by courtesy of the Trustees of the British Museum, and the Trustees for Roman Catholic Purposes; 56 reproduced by courtesy of the Trustees of the British Museum; 58 Fitzwilliam Museum, Cambridge; 60 by courtesy of the Board of Trustees of the Victoria and Albert Museum; 62 *Universal Penman*, Dover Publications; 92 reproduced by courtesy of the Trustees of the British Museum; 126 Rudolf Koch *The Book of Signs*, Dover Publications (runes).

The author would like to say a special thank you to all the contributors who made this book possible, to Sally and Antony for their support, and to Bill for taking the pictures.

I would also like to thank my teachers (Ann Camp in particular) and my students; the authors whose books are listed in the bibliography; my family and friends for their love and patience; and Veronica, who handed me an italic fountain pen on the fourth evening of a three-day week, when I first discovered, by candlelight, the lure of the edged pen.

FURTHER READING

If this book has whetted your appetite, you will want to refer to further, more specialized books; those that have been particularly helpful and interesting to me are listed below.

Techniques
Angel Marie *Painting for Calligraphers* Pelham Books 1984
Camp Ann *Pen Lettering* A & C Black 1984 (USA: Taplinger)
Child Heather ed. *The Calligrapher's Handbook* A & C Black 1985 (USA: Taplinger)
Child Heather ed. *Formal Penmanship and Other Papers* Lund Humphries (USA: Taplinger)
Harvey Michael *Lettering Design* Bodley Head 1975
Itten Johannes *The Art of Color* Rheinhold Publishing Co.
Johnston Edward *Writing, Illuminating and Lettering* A & C Black (USA: Taplinger)
Parkinson Andrew *Pens and Calligraphy* Rexel
Pearce Charles *The Little Manual of Calligraphy* Collins (USA: Taplinger)

History
Alexander J. J. G. *The Decorated Letter* Thames & Hudson 1978
Backhouse Janet *The Illuminated Manuscript* Phaidon 1979
Fairbank Alfred *A Book of Scripts* Faber 1979
Gray Nicolete *Lettering as Drawing* Oxford University Press 1971 (USA: Taplinger)
Jackson Donald *The Story of Writing* Trefoil (USA: Taplinger)
Knight Stan *Historical Scripts* A & C Black 1984

Special interest
Child Heather *Decorative Maps* Studio Vista
Child Heather *Heraldic Design* Bell & Hyman Ltd 1979
Thomson George *Rubber Stamps* Canongate Press

Compilations
Briem G.S.E. *Sixty Alphabets* Thames & Hudson
Rees Ieuan and Gullick Michael *Modern Scribes and Lettering Artists* Trefoil Books
International Calligraphy Today Thames & Hudson